# FALL IN,

*Selected*

D1586877

landscapes of his boy. Sussex Regiment in 1915, serving in France and Fland. His collection *The Shepherd* (1922) made his reputation as a poet; his classic account of his military service, *Undertones of War* (1928), was written while he was teaching in Japan. He made his living by writing and editing, with two extended periods of teaching: as a Fellow of Merton College 1931–42, and as Professor of English at the University of Hong Kong 1953–64. He received the Queen's Gold Medal for Poetry in 1956, and was Professor of Poetry at the University of Oxford 1966–68. His passions were poetry, book collecting, cricket, and the English countryside; he was haunted by his war experience all his life.

Robyn Marsack began her long association with Carcanet Press by editing Edmund Blunden's *Selected Poems* in 1982, and worked as a publishers' editor until she became Director of the Scottish Poetry Library in 2000. She continues to write articles and reviews, and occasionally translates from French. She has co-edited several poetry anthologies, including *Oxford Poets 2013* with Iain Galbraith.

FyfieldBooks aim to make available some of the great classics of British and European literature in clear, affordable formats, and to restore often neglected writers to their place in literary tradition.

FyfieldBooks take their name from the Fyfield elm in Matthew Arnold's 'Scholar Gypsy' and 'Thyrsis'. The tree stood not far from the village where the series was originally devised in 1971.

> *Roam on! The light we sought is shining still.*
> *Dost thou ask proof? Our tree yet crowns the hill,*
> *Our Scholar travels yet the loved hill-side*

from 'Thyrsis'

*Edmund Blunden*

# FALL IN, GHOSTS

*Selected War Prose*

Edited with an introduction by
*Robyn Marsack*

Fyfield*Books*

CARCANET

First published in Great Britain in 2014 by
Carcanet Press Limited
Alliance House
Cross Street
Manchester M2 7AQ

www.carcanet.co.uk

A CIP catalogue record for this book is available from the British
Library

ISBN 978 1 84777 211 4

The publisher acknowledges financial assistance from
Arts Council England

Typeset by XL Publishing Services, Exmouth
Printed and bound in England by SRP Ltd, Exeter

# CONTENTS

## Chapter 2.

### ENTRY OF THE GLADIATORS

That curious procession, the Transport, was on its way up, and ensconced somewhere in it were two people who anticipated the very worst. On the horizon in front casual yellow lights climbed up broadening, leered maliciously and expired: there were long bursts of machine-gun fire: down south a straſe was warming up and a sinister thudding made itself heard and, even at this distance of perhaps a dozen miles, felt in the air. Through the shutting darkness a low damp wind came whispering, causing D—— to murmur something about unshriven spirits, and a facetious driver to bawl, "Wind favourable for whizzbangs tonight Will?" Will, however, had sunk into a hypnotic doze behind his monotonous trotting mules, and made no answer. The column rattled ahead without any obstruction (those were halcyon days for the

12

A page from Blunden's manuscript of *De Bello Germanico*. Reproduced from facsimile, courtesy of the Estate of Edmund Blunden.

# INTRODUCTION

Edmund Blunden's battalion nickname, 'Rabbit', his characterisation of himself at the end of his best-selling memoir *Undertones of War* as 'a harmless young shepherd in a soldier's coat', and the frequent descriptions by friends of his 'birdlike' aspect suggest a man ill-equipped to deal with the privations and horrors of front-line service in France 1916–18. Or indeed with the social demands on an officer at the Front, as he indicates with characteristic self-deprecation:

> 'Have a drink?' 'No thanks, I don't drink.' 'Have a ciga-
> rette?' 'No thanks, I don't smoke.' 'Play bridge?' 'Sorry,
> I don't play cards.' 'Well, what the hell *do* you do?' No
> known heading apparently applied to me.

*De Bello Germanico* and the essays collected here show us a man who never lost sight of that teenager who set out for France, and whose imaginative life was shaped by his army years. It shaped his physical life, too, which mostly goes unmentioned: asthma exacerbated by gassing, breathless-ness, war nightmares that disturbed his sleep throughout his life, and – not surprisingly – ready recourse to alcohol. A crude description of Blunden's trajectory would be that he started out in Paradise, tumbled into Hell, and spent the remainder of his life between the two, but it would have to be complicated by the knowledge that the hellish years provided some of his proudest memories ('I knew that I did better one or two nights on the River Ancre than I ever can with my ink bottle'[1]), his most enduring friendships; the essays are a testament to all that.

Edmund Blunden was born in London on 1 November 1896, to Charles and Georgina Blunden; they had met when he was head teacher of St John's primary school, Fitzroy Square, and she was starting out as a teacher. With Edmund and his baby sister they moved to Yalding in Kent in 1898, and this village remained his ideal: 'How I turned to you / Beyond estranging years that cloaked my view / with all their wintriness of fear and strain…'.[2] His happy childhood there was succeeded by stimulating schooldays at Christ's Hospital in Horsham, where he was eventually captain of the school and also captain of his house cricket team – the house being Coleridge A, one of the strong literary links that Blunden so treasured in the school. (S.T. Coleridge, Charles Lamb and Leigh Hunt were all pupils of Christ's Hospital.) In 1914 he was awarded a scholarship to read Classics at The Queen's College, Oxford, but he was bound for the army, joining up in August 1915.

His post-war life, in the period in which he was writing most of these essays, included his first marriage in 1918, his meeting Siegfried Sassoon in 1919 and the death of his first child, Joy, aged five weeks, the same year. He went up to Oxford in the autumn, changed his subject from Classics to English, moved to Boar's Hill outside the town where John Masefield, Robert Graves and Robert Nichols were also living, but found he was more interested in editing the poems of John Clare (1793–1864) than in following his course. It was also very hard for returned servicemen – as other memoirs relate – to adapt to life at Oxford, and he had a wife and family: Clare, born in 1920 and then John, in 1922. So he left Oxford after a year, and became assistant to John Middleton Murry on the *Athenaeum*. Between 1920 and 1924 he contributed over 200 pieces to the *Athenaeum* and the *Nation*, and with his contributions to the *Times Literary Supplement* and other journals, produced over 400 items in those years, as well as publishing his collections *The Waggoner* (1920), *The Shepherd and Other Poems of Peace and War* (1922), and his edition (with Alan Porter) of *Poems Chiefly from Manuscript* by John Clare.

A voyage to South America on a cargo ship in 1922 was intended to improve his health – he produced a prose account, *The Bonaventure* – but the strain of earning his living, supporting his family and finding that his wife did not enjoy the literary life he relished in London, led him to accept Robert Nichols's suggestion that he apply for the position of Professor of English in Tokyo, when Nichols retired in 1924. Mary and the children remained in England, and after a depressed start Blunden began to find Japan congenial, and worked on what was to become *Undertones of War.*

When he returned to England in 1928, he went back to literary journalism and again produced 400 contributions to journals over about three years, along with editions of various cherished poets' works. *Undertones of War* was published in 1928, and his collection *Near and Far*, with the much-anthologised poem 'Report on Experience', came out when he was 33:

> I have been young, and now am not too old;
> And I have seen the righteous forsaken,
> His health, his honour and his quality taken.
>     This is not what we were formerly told. […]

His marriage ended formally in 1931; in the same year he published his edition of *The Poems of Wilfred Owen*, which was to remain standard for many years, and became a Fellow and Tutor in English at Merton College, Oxford.[3] There he remained until 1942, and during those years met, married and divorced the writer Sylva Norman. In 1932 they visited the French battlefields around Cassel, Amiens and the Somme, and co-wrote a 'novel' of the trip which Blunden's biographer describes as probably Blunden's 'least distinguished literary venture',[4] *We'll Shift our Ground* (1933). *The Mind's Eye*, a collection of essays, was published in 1934, as was a collection of poems, *Choice or Chance*.

Blunden resigned from Merton in 1942 and returned to work on the *TLS*. In 1945 he married Claire Poynting, fifteen years his junior, with whom he had four daughters and much happiness. In a loving but also a warning letter, Blunden told her that the lists of those killed in World War II brought to mind his comrades through a coincidence of names:

> I find the name of Guy Compton, who was in my company in 1916 and who was an extraordinarily brave youth; he left us and was killed in 1917. I can still see him and hear him returning from bombing a German trench and (to his own horror) killing a poor old spectacled fellow who was creeping round a corner with awful anxiety. So you see how the years pass, for I am really not much more fit for this world than I was when I gave Compton a drink and listened to his passionate and half-weeping story. That was at 'Port Arthur', which I haunt still (perhaps they don't know what it is, at the estaminet there, that disturbs the silence).[5]

That same haunting is lightly sketched in 'The Extra Turn', where Blunden imagines a gramophone still playing 'If You Were the Only Girl in the World' at Auchonvilliers, long after the British soldiers have departed. The turntable never ceases: the war itself keeps revolving in the listener's mind. In *The Mind's Eye*, Blunden writes as one to whom a calendar date means nothing: 'the baffling of my sense of time present' takes only a song.[6]

The last essay in this collection was published in 1968, in a volume to commemorate the fiftieth anniversary of the end of the war, by which time Blunden was settled in his final home in Long Melford, Suffolk. He had been Professor of English at the University of Hong Kong 1953–64, and in 1966 had been elected as Professor of Poetry at Oxford, succeeding Robert Graves in a much-publicised vote (his closest rival was Robert Lowell). But in 1968 he resigned for health reasons, and this essay was one of his last to be published. Blunden also wrote a piece for the *Daily Express* for the armistice, in which he considered

whether 'the effect of the Old War would lose its impris-
oning power', given that since 1918 'hardly a day or night
passed without my losing the present and living in a ghost
story'. He had once thought it might, about a year previously when he and other old soldiers and their friends had
visited the battlefields. He had been pointing out aspects of
the Ypres Salient, and

> had the sensation that suddenly, after so long, the obsti-
> nate scenes were at last vanishing. It was as though I was
> looking at a countryside where there had never been any
> war. Even the enormous Messines mine crater, which is
> just one of the effects of Ypres, no longer demanded my
> notice. [...] And yet, even as I think of that incredible
> war work, it stops any question of forgetting. I know, now
> that I am an old man, that I take with me something that
> will never yield to the restoratives of time.[7]

What did it mean, then, to survive? Undoubtedly
Blunden suffered from what is now called post-traumatic
stress disorder: guilt at surviving, and not being with his
battalion on the Somme in 1918 ('Why slept not I in Flanders clay / With all the murdered men?')[8]; endless
revisitation of the battlefields, in dreams and on paper;
difficulties in close relationships – Blunden was benevolent
towards but not deeply engaged with his young second
family; an unyielding sense of responsibility to the dead.
Whatever he could or might do – and as in his Hong Kong
tenure, he tried to fend off the disorder by over-working –
it never seemed to be enough.

Of the First World War poets best known to us a hundred
years later, Blunden spent the longest period of continuous
service in the Front Line: twenty-four months, without
being wounded. Edward Thomas was in France for only
four months before his death at Arras; Charles Sorley and
Julian Grenfell both died in 1915 after less than a year of

service; Robert Graves served for a year before injuries and ill-health kept him in England; Ivor Gurney was sent back to England, suffering from the effects of gas, in 1917 after about fourteen months in France; Siegfried Sassoon served sixteen months; Isaac Rosenberg nineteen months before his death in spring 1918. David Jones survived the opening of the Battle of the Somme, was wounded but back in action in October 1916, and after twenty-two months was sent home with trench fever. He died in 1974, the same year as Blunden.

Four of those five surviving poets wrote their memoirs of the war: Blunden's *Undertones of War* came first, reprinted three times within a month of its publication on the tenth anniversary of the end of the war. Sassoon's *Memoirs of a Fox-Hunting Man* (1928) was followed by *Memoirs of an Infantry Officer* (1930); between them came Graves's *Goodbye to All That*, which infuriated both Blunden and Sassoon. They spent an enraged evening annotating a copy 'with over 300 corrections and hostile comments in the margin', which they intended to deposit in the British Museum. Blunden's relationship with Graves did not mend for nearly forty years. Writing to the Keats scholar Takeshi Saito in Japan, Blunden excoriated his former friend: 'It is the season of gross and silly war books, and he has succeeded in selling his. [...] the distortion of men like Graves has been so widely commended; it is like using the cemeteries which crowd the old line of battle from north to south as latrines.'[9]

Jones was also working on his interpretation of the war in 1927, but *In Parenthesis* was not published until 1937. It is interesting to set his 'writing' (he does not label it as prose or poetry) beside Blunden's, so different in kind – modernist beside modern – yet arising from the same deeply felt comradely and commemorative impetus. Jones's Preface begins 'THIS WRITING IS FOR MY FRIENDS...': 'it looks like a war memorial and sounds like a poem', as Jon Stallworthy comments.[10] The title of the first part is 'THE MANY MEN SO BEAUTIFUL' from

Coleridge's *Rime of the Ancient Mariner*, a poem that Blunden also keeps returning to:

> The many men so beautiful
> And they all dead did lie:
> And a thousand thousand slimy things
> Lived on; and so did I.

Perhaps it was partly as a riposte to Graves that Blunden resurrected his 'fragment of trench history', as well as wanting to help his younger brother, Gilbert. Blunden has left barely a trace of *De Bello Germanico*'s composition. A manuscript copy exists, sixty-odd pages written in his beautiful hand on small sheets of notepaper with the crest of the Royal Sussex regiment, and not one crossing-out or amendment (see example on page vi). The writing becomes more cramped as Blunden continues, whether in haste or because of limited paper supplies there is no way of knowing. Neither can we tell whether this is a fair copy, made for his brother for typesetting clarity, or whether he composed it in just this form. It was pointed out to me that when Blunden took his turn writing the Battalion's war diary in October 1917, he was able to make his entries without alteration under the most difficult circumstances, so perhaps this handwritten text (now in the Echenberg War Poetry Collection) is indeed the first and only draft.

Gilbert Blunden's Preface states that the manuscript had 'slept with cobwebs and dust' since 1918, when it had been 'interrupted by the unnerved state into which the country fell'. 'Unnerved' is a very distinctive adjective for the atmosphere around the time of the Armistice: would that have been Blunden's judgement rather than his brother's? There were 250 copies printed on ordinary paper, priced at 15 shillings, measuring 7½ × 5 inches, and 25 slightly larger copies (8 × 5½ inches) on 'special paper' with a leather spine and corners, priced at two guineas. There is only a passing reference to *De Bello Germanico* in the published correspondence between Blunden and Siegfried Sassoon.

Sassoon mentions receiving a copy in a letter of 24 October 1930, but any comment on it goes unrecorded.[11]

Blunden probably did not have it with him in Japan where, relying on memory and a couple of maps, he wrote his second prose assay, 'going over the ground again', as he knew he would always. He was dismissive of *De Bello Germanico* in the 'Preliminary' to *Undertones of War*:

> I tried once before. True, when events were not yet ended, and I was drifted into a backwater. But what I then wrote, and little enough I completed, although in its details not much affected by the perplexities of distancing memory, was noisy with a depressing forced gaiety then very much the rage. To call a fellow creature 'old bean' may be well and good; but to approach in the beanish style such mysteries as Mr Hardy forthshadowed in *The Dynasts* is to have misunderstood, and to pull Truth's nose. (*Undertones*, p. xli)

Readers now will scarcely accuse Blunden of 'the beanish style'; the account has a vivacity that seems neither 'forced' nor 'depressing' but wonderfully composed – in both senses of the word, both artful and astonishingly serene. It is hard to believe that it was written by a man of twenty-two, immediately after the war.

It begins *in medias res*, in contrast to *Undertones'* considered opening declaration 'I was not anxious to go'. Here there is no hint of volition: men are sent like parcels at the direction of an unseen hand. The reader arrives in Béthune alongside the innocent abroad, and there is Dickensian brio in the narrator's immediate encounters: the 'betabbed encyclopaedia' directing them, the misinformation, the chaos, the men ribbing the conductor, all in contrast to the preceding night's 'singularly horrible counterfeit sleep'. Blunden's adjectives – 'gilded but scorbutic youth' (suffering from scurvy, so both decorated and yellow) – have a nineteenth-century tang, and this alerts us to his mindset. Here is a sheltered boy of nineteen, brought up in a country schoolmaster's household, well-schooled at Christ's Hospital, in love with the literature of the eighteenth and nineteenth centuries: this is the lens through which he views his experience. It is not pastiche or decoration but thoroughly absorbed reading that surfaces in these verbal flourishes, which decrease and alter as the account continues. Allied to this reading, inseparable from it, is the observant countryman, whose first, relieved thought is that the French fields had 'a harmless, parcelled, thrifty look'. It is out of this conjunction (close reading and close observation) and disjunction – between the mental and spiritual sustenance they provide, and the circumstances in which he now reads and observes – that Blunden makes his prose and poetry.

In his influential study *The Great War and Modern Memory*, Paul Fussell maintains that Blunden's archaisms, the rhetorical questions and exclamations 'reveal a mind playing over a past felt to be not at all military or political but only literary' – not quite the case, as is clear from Blunden's references to the Duke of Marlborough's campaigns, for example; he is very conscious that these lands have been contested before. Yet it is literary tradition that matters most to him, and Fussell pinpoints exactly where literary tradition and landscape meet in a brilliantly perceptive paragraph:

> But archaism is more than an overeducated tic in Blunden. It is directly implicated in his meaning. With language as with landscape, his attention is constantly on pre-industrial England, the only repository of criteria for measuring fully the otherwise unspeakable grossness of the war. [...] Blunden's style is his critique. It suggests what the modern world would look like to a sensibility that was genuinely civilized.[12]

What experience could the teenaged Blunden bring to the war but his sensibility, soaked in literature? And afterwards, it was the war that seeped through everything. There was a powerful tension between the need to communicate – imperative, because otherwise the dead were betrayed – and the impossibility of the 'civilised' sensibility finding a way to describe the war. Authors ranging from Edith Wharton, D.H. Lawrence and Henry James to Walter Benjamin and Sigmund Freud are summoned by the critic Randall Stevenson to attest to the 'unspeakable' nature of the war. He quotes from Hugh MacDiarmid's poem 'Talking with Five Thousand People in Edinburgh', where MacDiarmid castigates teachers, ministers and writers for living off a decomposed vocabulary, 'Big words that died over twenty years ago/ – For most of the important words were killed in the First World War'.[13] In *De Bello*, Blunden downplays with his choice of noun one aspect of front-line existence: 'The great *defect* of war here as elsewhere was the shortage of sleep…', whereas at about the same point in the narrative of *Undertones*, he elaborates, looking back on this 'profound tiredness' to compare it with the battalion's feeling in 1918, 'almost mad for sleep' under the German offensive Blunden had escaped:

> Imagine their message; they will never open their mouths, unless perhaps one hour, when the hooded shape comes to call them away, they lift from the lips of their extremest age a terrible complaint and courage, in phrases sounding to the bystanders like the 'drums and tramplings' of a mad dream. (*Undertones*, p. 34)[14]

And if the vocabulary for this experience were to be found, would the public want to read such accounts? Ford Madox Ford remarked presciently in 1915: 'Everyone will want to forget it – it will be bad form to mention it.'[15] When Blunden refers to the 'unnerved' state of the country, perhaps he means this lack of willingness to learn and feel what the war had been like for the combatants, and this attitude, too, must have dissuaded him from continuing his account. *De Bello* ends, appropriately enough, with a dog left behind, 'the very image of misery'.

As well as finding an adequate vocabulary, there was the impossibility of providing an over-arching narrative, and in *De Bello* Blunden does not attempt this. At the end of Chapter VIII of *Undertones* there is a brilliant passage conveying the 'succession of sensations erratically' occupying Blunden's mind, and this evocation of the incoherence and chaos of war could perhaps only have been achieved with the passage of time. Stallworthy, in comparing *De Bello* to *Undertones*, suggests that the former is 'not so much revised as shaken like a kaleidoscope' to make the latter, 'its bright fragments being incorporated into a larger and richer pattern'.[16] There was a tension between being true to sensation and to the framework of the action, but the individual's perception was the counter to 'official' accounts, to newspaper reports: it had the desired stamp of authenticity. Even when Blunden turns to providing 'A Battalion History' in 1933, it remains particular; while war historians warned of the limitations of accounts by individuals, they had to admit that 'on a modern battlefield [...] knowledge of events is extraordinarily local'.[17]

Ford wrote, in a manuscript fragment, about the impossibility of describing the war in general:

Today, when I look at a mere coarse map of the Line, simply to read 'Ploegsteert' or 'Armentières' seems to bring up extraordinarily coloured and exact pictures behind my eyeballs [...] of towers, and roofs, and belts of trees and sunlight; or, for the matter of these, of men, burst into mere showers of blood, and dissolving into muddy ooze; or of aeroplanes and shells against the translucent blue. – But, as for putting them – into words! No: the mind stops dead, and something in the brain stops and shuts down [...][18]

His biographer, Alan Judd, suggests that to the outsider, 'the setting seems, perhaps misleadingly, to be of the essence [... but Ford's] subject was not war but the people, the people war produced'.

Landscape was central to Blunden's perception by upbringing, and was reinforced by literature, but what the war gave him was experience of a vast range of people, and he felt very keenly his duty to them. He tended not to describe the body, simply – there is no hint of homoeroticism in his work – but the body in motion and as it expressed the spirit, in gesture and in speech. In *De Bello* he uses initials, having no permission to do otherwise; in *Undertones* he uses names: this is their memorial. Randall Stevenson suggests that the names of people and places gave a kind of solidity to experience, something to hold on to; yet the names of places were two-edged. Blunden shows this in 'Trench Nomenclature', at first with relish, and then with a terrible dismay: 'Genius named them, as I live! What but genius could compress / In a title what man's humour said to man's supreme distress? [...] Ah, such names and apparitions! name on name! what's in a name? / From the fabled vase the genie in his cloud of horror came.'

Describing damage to place was a way of conveying the juxtaposition remarked on by every war writer: the endurance, even the loveliness of nature – of culture, sometimes, where farmland survived – and the denaturing force of constant bombardment, of the endless movement of men and machines. Blunden's essay 'War and Peace' is a concentrated evocation of 'Nature as then disclosed in fits and starts', prologue to the epic drama. It has the density of poetry, adjectives working hard: 'our restless camps' – both always packing up and re-settling, and in themselves providing scant rest for the men; 'the dark unfruiting clay' – nothing grows in it, of course, but later readers hear an echo of Wilfred Owen's 'Futility': 'Was it for this the clay grew tall?'; 'snow untidily tenanted' by old soldiers; the 'streaming hazels' in a storm. This was written in Japan, 'And if this winter is not contrary to the last, I shall often seem to be in Flanders...'.

*Undertones* ends with Blunden's departure from the

trenches, and his last sight of the countryside near Ancre, asking whether it could have been 'more sweetly at rest', 'more incapable of dreaming a field-gun?' He answers his own question: it was to be blown to bits, but he did not anticipate that, still too young to know the war's 'depth of ironic cruelty'. 'Aftertones' gives us the sequel, Blunden's return to France post-Armistice, and it is a painful account of privations and divisions, of dishonesty and the disappearance of *esprit de corps*, of 'a fantastic chivalry'. The melancholy of these articles about 'going over the ground' – 'The Somme Still Flows', 'We Went to Ypres' have a slightly longer perspective – contrasts with the happiness that suffuses 'Fall In, Ghosts', despite the deaths and losses it recalls.

Hew Strachan, in his introduction to a recent edition of *Undertones*, remarks that Blunden 'increasingly romanticized the memory which his own writings did so much to keep alive' (p.xi). Yet the tendency to do so had been there from the outset: in *De Bello* he says of his very first night at the Front, 'so early had my love for my new battalion taken root'. In her thought-provoking study *Modernism, Male Friendship, and the First World War*, Sarah Cole quotes from the military historian B.H. Liddell Hart:

> Now, the war, at any rate on the Western Front, was waged by Battalions, not by individuals, by bands of men who, if the spirit were right, lived in such intimacy that they became part of one another. The familiar phrase, 'a happy Battalion,' has a deep meaning, for it symbolises that fellowship of the trenches which was such a unique and unforgettable experience for all who ever shared in it, redeeming the sordidness and stupidity of war by a quickening of the sense of interdependence and sympathy.[19]

This is a feeling expressed by many memoir-writers of the

period: that their most meaningful relationship was with the battalion – 'There had never been mutual understanding like it in your experience', Blunden boasts – although the sense of an enclosed male community might have its precedent in English public schools. Cole differentiates between 'friendship', put under so much pressure by the hazards of war, and distinguished by affinities and choice, and 'comradeship', created by the circumstances of war, in which commitment is to the group rather than the individual. What bound the men was, in the opinion of Robert Graves and fellow officers, 'regimental pride'. They agreed it was 'the strongest moral force that kept a battalion going as an effective fighting unit; contrasting it particularly with patriotism and religion'.[20] Yet, as Blunden found, the battalion itself could dissolve in a few days' action, as happened to his own on the Somme in 1916. Cole quotes Sassoon:

> All I knew was that I'd lost my faith in [both home life and the war] and there was nothing left to believe in except 'the Battalion spirit' [...] But while exploring my way into the War I had discovered the impermanence of its humanities. One evening we could all be together in a cosy room [...] A single machine-gun or a few shells might wipe out the whole picture within a week.[21]

Blunden accepts this, in 'Fall In, Ghosts', but the battalion remains 'his rock':

> Some faces seemed destined to go on for ever, for a battalion could not be suffered by whatever powers then ruled the mad hour to be quite extinguished or supplanted. In them was concentrated, after the frightful desolations of battle upon battle, the beauty, faith, hope which flowered in the word: the battalion. Or was this an illusion? Very few men lived through the full career of any unit (that perhaps is the more scientific term); and, as those familiar faces became more remote, others

became the typical, life-giving, and sustaining presences with – was it the same battalion? It had the same number and place in the line. It was thought the same; but, perhaps, each of us knew a battalion not quite identical with any other man's […] We come together, once a year, without allusion to the details of our own former shares of the history that concerns us, and we reanimate – the battalion. It is our quaint attempt at catching a falling star.

As his composite account of the battalion reunion progresses, Blunden brings in the ghosts of men that did not survive, but the boundary between the two companies is almost invisible. Cole quotes from 'The Homecoming' by Joseph Lee: 'A *dead man shall stand* / *At each live man's hand* – / *For they also have come home*',[22] a testament to the psychic effect of the war though not, of course, to the actuality, with so many bodies left in cemeteries. 'At what point do we separate from those other listeners I have named?' Blunden asks.

The post-war world apparently did want to know about the war after all, a decade afterwards, yet it was still, for many, an 'incommunicable' experience. Webb describes Blunden encountering an incoming batsman at a cricket match who 'complained that he had written about the war "like a child who was happy with a bag of sweets"'.[23] But there were many letters from writers, soldiers, even a German officer, thanking him for what he had done in *Undertones of War*; one in particular he treasured from an ex-private in the Northumberland Fusiliers:

To really understand your book one must have gone through the mill as an infantryman. […] I must tell you how much I enjoyed your book, and the very odd feeling that came over me. I cannot properly express it here. I am just an ordinary working man.[24]

*De Bello* is full of the voices of working men, more immediately so than *Undertones*.[25]

What else could Blunden do for the dead? Reluctantly, given his deep-seated antipathy to Kipling, he agreed to succeed him as literary advisor to the Imperial War Graves Commission, and that meant revisiting the battlefields and cemeteries on a regular basis. In an introduction to Philip Longworth's *The Unending Vigil: A History of the Commonwealth War Graves Commission* (1967), Blunden wrote that as they commemorated those who had 'died for their friends', the cemeteries were 'in a sense the poetry of that action'.[26]

For decades, it was the poetry itself that he preserved and presented. Concentrating on his war experience, I have not included here a series of introductions and prefaces to anthologies of war poetry, to individual collections, or excerpts from his pamphlet for the British Council series 'Writers & their Works'. *War Poets 1914–1918*, first published in 1958, was still available over twenty years later (with an updated bibliography), with its canonical progress from Brooke to Owen. Throughout his life he edited the works of eighteenth- and nineteenth-century authors, major and minor, but his editions of Wilfred Owen in 1931 and of Ivor Gurney in 1954 were landmarks. Dominic Hibberd has suggested that Blunden 'probably had more influence than anyone on the modern view of 1914–18 verse' though his work as editor and critic.[27]

'Over there are faith, life, virtue in the sun' concludes 'Report on Experience': faith, virtue, courage, honour – these 'big words' did not lose their meaning for Blunden in 1914; rather, his war service deepened their meaning. A hundred years later, it is harder for many readers to grasp that than to appreciate the justifiable rage and cynicism of other writers.[28] Blunden – unassuming, hardworking, courteous, intelligently discriminating – honoured his comrades in the art, the soldier-poets he felt understood the war best, and in his writings kept faith with all the dead.

> *Yea, how they set themselves in battle-array*
> *I shall remember to my dying day.*

I am grateful for the assistance and encouragement of Stuart Airlie, Margi Blunden, Martin Chown and Helen Tookey in preparing this collection. It is not my book to dedicate, but let me remember here two men who served in the New Zealand Expeditionary Force: my grandfather, Charles Croft Marsack (1892–1987), who wrote a humorous poem about 'Minnies' and a lyrical one about poppies, as well as a vivid diary of his months at the Front at the time of Passchendaele; and his life-long friend, our 'Uncle' David Ramsay Mansfield (1892–1979).

Robyn Marsack

# TIMELINE OF BLUNDEN'S WAR

Not all of the Battalion's movements are recorded here; the broad outline is adapted from the detailed one provided by Martin Chown in his companion guide to *Undertones of War*, with his kind permission.

August 1915–April 1916
In training camps at Weymouth, Shoreham; near Cork. To Boulogne, a day's training at Etaples and then up the line. At this period the British held the front line from Ypres to the Somme, and the 11th Sussex were about halfway between the two.

May 1916
9th, from Béthune to Le Touret; 14th, relieved 13th Royal Sussex at Festubert; 28th, ordered to front line at Cuinchy; EB to three-day gas school at Essars.

June 1916
11th, relieved by Argyll and Sutherland Highlanders, returned to Hingette; 16th, to Croix Barbée, north of Richebourg; 28th, relieved by Cambridgeshires, to Richebourg.

July 1916
1st, relieved to Lacouture orchards; 7th, relieved 4th King's Liverpools at Auchy-les-Mines for about a week, then back to Le Touret; 20th, holding Ferme du Bois line; 24th, holding Festubert breastworks; 29th, relieved to Le Touret and then Béthune.

August 1916
Returned to trenches at Givenchy; 11th, began the journey to the Somme; 27th, reached Mailly Wood.

September 1916
3rd, attack began. Battalion relieved by Cheshires and reassembled at Hamel: reduced from 4 to 2 companies, with the loss of

300 men; 6th, moved to Beaussart, received nearly 500 reinforcements from England; 14th, to Beaumont Hamel trenches;
26th–27th, battalion involved in final capture of Thiepval.

October 1916
4th, relieved by 14th Hants. The Battalion held a front usually
held by two battalions for 10 days, and had been in the front line
for three weeks. 16th, relieved by Royal Navy Division, but
straight to Authuille Wood south of Thiepval; 21st, having fought
for five weeks without rest, advanced over open ground to take
Stuff Trench (Battle of Ancre Heights); cost 274 killed, wounded
and missing. 25th, after a few days' relief, returned to the line at
Thiepval Wood; 30th, moved to Schwaben Redoubt.

November 1916
1st, relieved by the 6th Cheshires; 3rd, back to Thiepval Wood;
10th, after a few days' rest at Senlis, back to Schwaben Redoubt;
13th–18th, final offensive of Battle of the Somme; 18th, to
Poperinghe; 28th, end of train journey to M Camp on the Poperinghe–Watou Road.

December 1916
5th, after training and refitting at M Camp, to Moulle to build
rifle ranges; 15th, to Canal Bank trenches; 23rd, to E Camp in
Elverdinghe Woods; 28th, relieved 10th South Wales Borderers
at Boesinghe trenches.

January 1917
14th, through the Menin Gate to relieve trenches at Potizje; 18th,
returned to Ypres basements; 24th, back to relieve 14th Hants in
Potizje; 26th, EB's Military Cross gazetted; 28th, relieved by 14th
Hants, returned to Ypres.

February 1917
In camp at Vlamertinghe, and at Winnipeg Camp, for reorgani-
sation and specialist training; 25th, occupied trenches at
Obervatory Ridge.

March 1917
Battalion goes to and fro between Observatory Ridge and
Winnipeg Camp.

April 1917
To infantry barracks at Ypres, trenches at Hill Top Farm, back to
Canal Bank and M Camp.

May 1917
Transferred to Wormhoudt (north of Cassel), then to D camp in
the Elverdinghe Woods where the battalion helped to build railways.

June 1917
Held trenches at Hill Top, with a break at Canal Bank; 21st, to
Houlle for three weeks' training.

July 1917
To C Camp at Elverdinghe, now under bombardment; 28th to
trenches at Hill Top to prepare for attack on 31st, part of the
Flanders offensive.

August 1917
1st–3rd, attack continued; relieved at night, 275 casualties; to
School Camp, beyond Poperinghe; 21st, to Spoil Bank and then
Ridge Wood Camp; 27th, relieved Black Watch at Hollebeke.

September 1917
Held the line at Mount Sorrell; four days in Larch Wood Tunnels;
24th, occupied front line south of Menin Road; 25th–27th,
fighting and intense shelling, casualties estimated at 200; 28th,
rest at Mt Kokereele.

October 1917
15th, on the way back to the front, shell dropped among HQ
staff; 16th–20th, two nights in the Tunnels, three in front line
south of Tower Hamlets; 23rd, transferred to old horse lines near
Rheninghelst; 29th, to more salubrious Chippewa Camp.

November 1917
8th–25th, return to Chippewa Camp after Tower Hamlets and
Vierstraat; to Bedford House near Ypres, at the end of the month
building railway and causeway.

December 1917
EB on signalling course for two months at Mont des Cats.

January 1918
Held mud holes at Westroosebeek, then to Hill Top Farm, School Camp.

February 1918
To Battlefield of Cambrai and ruins of Gouzeaucourt as close support and firing line. 21st, EB sent back to England for six months' duty at a training centre in Suffolk.

The Battalion suffered 320 casualties in the retreat of March–April 1918, although some reported as missing had in fact been taken prisoner. They returned to the Ypres Salient, and in June 1918 were divided, some acting as instructors to the American forces and some returned to England. On 17 October the newly constituted battalion left from Scotland for northern Russia.

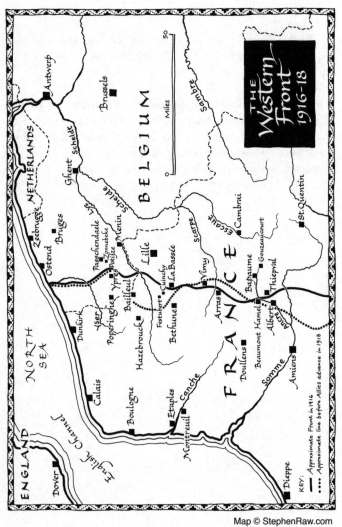

THE Western Front 1916-18

Miles 50

ENGLAND

NORTH SEA

English Channel

Dover

Dieppe

Calais

Boulogne

Étaples

Montreuil

Canche

Dunkirk

Zeebrugge

Ostend

Bruges

NETHERLANDS

Antwerp

Brussels

BELGIUM

Ghent

Scheldt

Sambre

Passchendaele

Poperinghe

Ypres

Zonnebeke

Zillebeke

Menin

Yser

Hazebrouck

Bailleul

Lille

Béthune

Festubert

Cuinchy

La Bassée

Vimy

Scarpe

Arras

Cambrai

St. Quentin

Escaut

Bapaume

Gouzeaucourt

Thiepval

Beaumont Hamel

Albert

Ancre

Somme

Doullens

Amiens

FRANCE

KEY:
— Approximate Front in 1916
•••• Approximate line before Allies advance in 1918

Map © StephenRaw.com

# DE BELLO GERMANICO

## *The Publisher's Preface*

The following manuscript having come into my possession, I decided to make it the opening number in my present Publishing experiment.

I feel certain that those who have read and still treasure *Undertones of War* will enjoy the reading and possession of *De Bello Germanico*. The Author of *Undertones* refers to this manuscript in his introduction to that publication as if it ought not to have been written, but those who read it will find that such is not the case. Since 1918 it has slept with cobwebs and dust, and meanwhile the Author went to Japan and there wrote *Undertones*. But writing a new book does not mean that you can alter facts, and so we find *Undertones* and *De Bello Germanico* in complete understanding with each other. While *Undertones* has the mellowness of time and experience, this older story gives more attention to the very small detail which a young soldier was sure to notice, and indeed made his day and night. How many soldiers would not march fifteen miles rather than attend one General's Inspection, or wish for the Front Line rather than rest and training?

We can only regret that *De Bello Germanico* is not of greater length. It was interrupted by the unnerved state into which the country fell towards the end of 1918.

The title shows how recently the Author had read his Caesar; indeed, he carried a volume of *De Bello Gallico* with him as a soldier.

G.A. Blunden

# CHAPTER 1

## *Girding Our Loins*

Béthune. The long and slatternly train, scarcely in motion for the past twelve hours, stopped dead, and the carriages in succession gave that sudden backward mule-kick which gives troop-trains one of their unique charms, jolting us out of our singularly horrible counterfeit sleep. Yawning and rusty, we collected our trappings and jumped out on the track. I had no more idea than the man in the moon how far we were from the line – from one to thirty miles I decided! A few French porters and station-supporters, an already besieged Staff Captain, and vast numbers of innocents abroad like ourselves were collaborating in uproar, and several engines were artlessly shunting and shrieking alongside. Making sure of our valises we joined the avalanche with which the betabbed encyclopaedia was dealing, and later in the morning got to know that our objective was Locon and that the toy tramway would shortly take us there. We humped our valises, packs and lesser freights off the station, to find the steam car waiting across the street: but on learning that its departure would be later than sooner, D—, my companion, decided on a coffee first. As our informant was the driver of the car, a RE, this seemed a safe and seasonable plan; yet hardly had we begun on our 'elevenses' when a series of diabolical hootings warned us outside and we saw the iron monster (Ph. Gibbs) departing. Our goods were on board, and so we managed to catch up: but it was thus I became aware of the specious nature of the Sapper.

We now went rumbling and banging down a cobbled road (the first time I had seen this arrangement of light rail track alongside the highway), and learned with reassurance that Locon was not a hotbed of strife. The Tommies inside the car paraded much conventional wit about its speed, upholstery, and shape, and to my gratitude baited the conductor – 'Hey mate are we anywhere near Manchester?' ... 'Did you make it yourself?' ... 'Wot a shime robbin' the chile of 'is playtoy.' Their quota of good spirits was welcome after that angular night in the window-less carriage. Locon proved to be no great way off, and soon we were offloaded with our chattels at a sort of loft, varie-gated with chromatic signboards and legends, which was no less than the Brigade Office. Our next job was easy; our valises were lying in the mud and we sat on them 'pending the arrival of the Battalion Mess-cart', as pompously instructed by a gilded but scorbutic youth who rejoiced in three stars and tabs gorget. The day was dank and depressing.

Presently we were one each side of the mess-cart driver, 'going up to the line' – how often had I heard, and yet never really heard, the words before! The countryside had a harmless, parcelled, thrifty look; but my incipient idyllic view of war (hope fathering thought) was shattered by the driver, who said, 'Quartermaster were coming round this corner last night and Fritz sent over fifteen shells. Blew 'is 'orse onesided, one of 'em did.' This kept me ruminating awhile, through those rainy well-tilled lowlands checkered with red and white farms, colonnades of poplars and glis-tening shrines, till an instantaneous tremendous roar on our left nearly tumbled D— and myself out of the cart. The driver (one of the best of Sussex men, as I was to know better later on) was mildly amused, though the horse shied. ''Tis only a new six-inch battery, sir, our party have brought in.' I had thought it was the Boche throwing a medium earthquake at us: and resolved to avoid our own guns as much as the enemy's.

We now entered a hamlet, Le Touret, with one or two estaminets and a YMCA hut; and drove into a farmyard, where children and chicken peacefully engaged in the mud demonstrated how far we were from war's alarms. (The heavy guns fired over this and neighbour establishments.) Alighting, we were hailed in glucose, soothing tones by a Padre, who looked forth from a sort of horse-box. Yes, we were new officers joining the Battalion – would be awfully glad to come in and have a wash – no, we hadn't had tea. We were stoking up with generous spreads of Australian Quince and listening to the Padre's eulogy of certain officers (whom we later found to be like himself members of the Church of Rome) when the Quartermaster burst in upon us. He was the jolliest, kindliest old quartermaster that there could be anywhere – he made the little dingy room sparkle with good-natured wit and wisdom. 'Just been to see old Diamond-Dust (field cashier y'know). Pity you boys didn't get here earlier if you wanted some filthy lucre. Golly, there *were* some people in Béthune today – shouldn't be surprised if there isn't some dirty work coming off. I saw the girl in the boot-shop, Padre – she asked after you. Now you boys, plug in on that tea. Any time you want anything you ask the old Quarterbloke. [Encouraging wink] Why, Padre, haven't you stamped those letters yet? I say that new chestnut charger didn't half show his mettle today – nearly whizzed me into the Hotel de France – then he backed into some Japanese general's perambulator ...' We made a good tea, and cautiously enquired as to our fate.

'The Colonel wants you to go up with the rations tonight,' the Quartermaster remarked, somewhat brutally I thought, having hoped that the matter would be accomplished, like others in the Army, by easy stages. So far, however, apart from the heavy battery referred to, which occasionally bellowed, there was little noise or symptom of war. We took the air. With awe and his conversational laugh, which we later on found was successfully imitated by half the battalion, the Padre pointed out a litter of rusting ironware in a ditch, and informed us that these were old German bombs. This seemed a point of the first interest, but the interest evaporated when he told us in

gruesome tones that two transport men had been examining them last week when somehow one went off,
seriously wounding both. We now thought these bombs
should be interred and criticised anonymous authorities
for having failed to do it. Evidently a very slack war.
Farther down the road we met an officer who had trained
with us in England and arrived in France a fortnight before
ourselves. He vaguely recognised us with a Napoleonic
nod, and was greeted by genial D— with 'Well, how are
things, old thing?' 'Oh, not too bad back here,' conde-
scended the unshaven, clay-cased, and gumbooted one:
'but the line's hell.' He shed upon us two or three looks
intended to represent unspeakable memories of anguish
and horror: the mercury in my courage thermometer
dropped into the bulb. Our tragedian's remarks were now
aided and abetted by a sudden outburst of respectable
thunderclaps rending the none too distant air; 'Listen to
that … Christ! Fritz crumping Givenchy Keep again …
My God! it's hell.'

This officer had so imbued himself in highly-strung literature, as we remembered, that his soulful monologue lost
its savour, and old experience advising us that he would
now touch us for 'a small loan' unless we went, we went.
But we ran into another acquaintance, a cheerful man
whose more palatable opinions on the matter in hand we
eagerly expected.

'Hullo you fellows! Fancy you coming out!' (Not very
polite, this.) 'Your batt.'s holding the islands – round Canadian Orchard – went in night before last …' Was this a
maritime sector, I wondered? The mention of islands
certainly implied aquatic surroundings, and further allusions to 'the Duckboards' led me to imagine a kind of
archipelago with enclosures for ducks, no doubt piously
preserved by the troops until the return of their owners.
This chimera however, was dispelled by D— asking what
these islands and duckboards were; which our friend
answered by borrowing my notebook and making a sketch
thus: –

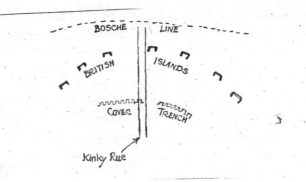

'You see,' he explained, 'the islands are only isolated posts, just about big enough for a small boy but his dog's tail would have to be showing. There are some duckboards between some of 'em but others you have to flounder through the mud to; anyway you can't move out or in by daylight.' 'Do you mean to say the War has been going on for all these months and we haven't got a communication trench up to the posts?' I murmured with certain qualms. 'Not a ruddy sign of one. Look here, man, I was going up that road the other night to see the posts and I suddenly realised there was nothing to stop the Hun slipping in between the islands and waiting for you. Then he opened up cross fire with two machine guns, bullets smacking up against the trees and ricocheting like hell-fire off the cobbles. I had to flop into the ditch and lie there sopped for twenty minutes while the lead was spacking all round. Well, so long, you chaps: jolly good luck.'

As we walked back brooding over the imminent nasti-ness of war, a microscopic hut built largely of biscuit tins, and displaying gorgeously wrapped CHOCOLAT POULAIN, silk cards, Venus pencils, Maryland cigarettes at 75 a franc and similar bright bargains, attracted us inside. We bought some Bouchées and Liqueur Chocolates all cautiously concealed in silver paper. The débitante, a well-favoured young lady with jet hair and eyes and the reddest of red cheeks, disclosed that she was a refugee, from Aubers (I confused this with E. A. Poe's Auber for a time), and was of opinion that 'M'sieu la guerre dure trop longtemps – zis war becomm too longh izzent he?'

Considering what we had just been hearing from a by no means hysterical source, and wondering whether we should be groping round uncharted alligator-holes by midnight ourselves, we very heartily concurred.

# CHAPTER 2
## *Entry of the Gladiators*

That curious procession, the Transport, was on its way up, and ensconced somewhere in it were two people who anticipated the very worst. On the horizon in front casual yellow lights climbed up broadening, leered maliciously and expired: there were long bursts of machine-gun fire; down south a strafe was warming up and a sinister thudding made itself heard and, even at this distance of perhaps a dozen miles, felt in the air. Through the shutting darkness a low damp wind came whispering, causing D— to murmur something about unshriven spirits, and a facetious driver to bawl, 'Wind favourable for whizzbangs tonight, Will?' Will, however, had sunk into a hypnotic doze behind his monotonous trotting mules, and made no answer. The column rattled ahead without any obstruction (those were halcyon days for the Transport). At last the Quartermaster, after seeing the convoy on the right road, left us to the mercies of the Transport Sergeant and departed with much good humour, spurring his animal, to take the CO up his 'Daily Prevaricator'. I was puffing along in my British Warm and pack, and was somewhat perturbed by the behaviour of the mules behind; they kept nosing forward by my shoulder to chat about something which I couldn't understand. No doubt they gathered I was a new draft. We passed a colony of half-ruined houses, with sacks stretched partway over some windows and lights glaring pleasantly from all. I was told these were the haunts of gunners, and miscellaneous outcries added the information that they were playing house.

Shortly after we turned on a side road and came across a kind of open-air smoking concert, standing or sitting in

groups, which now converged upon the waggons as they
drew up with cries of 'Transport up, boys!' and 'Any mail
tonight?' The social gathering having thus turned into a
Ration Party, the business of handing out mysterious sandbags – 'B Company Details', '23 Island', '12 Platoon Cover
Trench' – was hastily proceeded with: all were presently
piled aboard four low trucks on a light railway line, and
after domestic parleyings ('Had a letter from Char Muggins
today – he's a lucky bounder – in Eastbourne. Coo! some
people don't half seem to strike lucky …') good-nights were
exchanged and the emptied transport noisily made off for
Le Touret. We leant our shoulders to a ration truck and
started afresh. The simple-sounding matter of pushing a
truck along a trench tramway is rather complex on a dark
and/or dirty night. Special adroitness is necessary, and an
instinct for varying the length of one's pace, to keep step-
ping on the metal sleepers and to avoid the chasms
between. This cat-like tread, too frequently rewarded with
a barked shin, or bootfull of icy slime, must be combined
with frantic energy in propelling the truck, particularly on
wooden rails. Add to this, the probability of a sudden visitation of bullets or five-nines: which you are pensively
brooding on when your trolley jolts off the track or disap-
pears into a yawning pit in front, scattering its cargo. With
indescribable labour and language this is remedied and you
move on, when sudden looming figures with long strides
and short tempers begin to scuffle past and grimly remark
that the rest of the battalion's coming on behind. These
have barely passed, you are just congratulating yourself,
when an interminable stream of displeased and ejaculatory
Jocks repeat the act – coming off working party. There are
also people pushing trucks down the track … Yet even evil
journeys of this type have an end, and at last we came to
the tramhead. The rationeers shouldered their loads, over-
turned their trucks beside the track, and vanished through
the dark in different directions. We attached ourselves to
the Headquarters party, distinguished by their stock phrase
'O la la!'; and were led through an orchard and over two

foot-bridges, when I noticed three or four insects of an unfamiliar kind whip past with a whining 'Bizzz' – bullets! I bustled, and behold! we came under the lee of an apparently gigantic breastwork. Here I felt I should be able to study these random shots with more comfort; but first of all we had to report our arrival.

The Colonel, grey and evidently an Anglo-Indian, was sitting with the Adjutant, in a small sandbag hutch barely holding a rough table on which were a bowl of oranges, some maps, and three candles, all weaving winding-sheets. Ceiling and walls were decently veiled with canvas, behind which there seemed to be occasional scurryings, scratchings, and squeaks. The CO addressed us kindly but the Adjutant already eyed me with evident disesteem. From the Colonel's remarks it appeared that we were the saviours of the battalion, the first new officers since it came out two months earlier; D— was allotted to A Company and myself to C, who by great good fortune were in support. So we were given guides and once more tramped away. My temporary home was no great distance off, and after stumbling along various trenches I was urged through an aperture screened with sacking into a small and stuffy dugout. My new Company Commander, a fair-headed youth evidently no more than twenty years of age, but to my inward surprise possessing three stars, was in the middle of a profane argument with his three subalterns, and I hardly felt sure whether his 'Well, what the hell – ?' was in reference to his subject or my unlooked-for apparition. However, he elucidated my name and business, imparted those of himself and the other officers, and raised his voice in an elongated shriek 'Mess!' From without a hoarse responsive grunt was heard, with mutterings: and shortly a batman curiously like the Fat Boy in Pickwick, brought me in my first experience of Maconachie on an enamelled plate. Immediately forgetting what I had been trying to realise – namely that I was actually in a dugout at Festubert, that place of carnage – I 'fell to with an appetite'. The slight ripple of interest that my short-winded entry had caused swiftly died away, and a conversation which I found technical in the highest degree coruscated about me. Archibalds, Pushful Percies, The Mad Major, Baby Elephants, and many more minor characters of war flurried in masks and hoods before my mental vision – what could Pipsqueak mean anyway? and who was Minnie? These speculations were postponed by the Company Commander, who requested a pleasant, sleepy officer to take me 'round the works, sentries and all that', when I had finished my dinner. 'You can turn in when you get back my son,' he added to me. 'There's the bed; you'll probably have rats running across your dial about 2 ack emma but they're quite friendly really.' The bed indicated by him was a kind of burrow in the dugout wall, of sufficiently grisly appearance and a ratty odour. Two or three blankets and numerous sandbags were strewn over the floor, and I was glad to see a magazine or two with them. I finished my meal with some Californian Peaches (the first of a numerous race that later on fell victims to my rapacity in the trenches), and the inevitable trench savoury – singed sardines on toast. Drinks were to be had but I foolishly preferred 'lemonade', an acrid affair made of that powerful ration lime-juice, trench sugar (duly blended with tea), and chlorine-drugged water. Altogether, I began to feel the giant refreshed, and meekly informed my instructor L— that I was ready for the exhibition. Grousing a little at this unnatural disturbance, he proceeded to put on his cap and his revolver ('for those bloody rats' he explained) and we got out.

Standing still a few seconds to accustom his eyes to the dark, L— suddenly gripped my arm and, with his customary stammer, 'I say, look at that – look at that strafe! Brickstacks again; they cop out nearly every night. Charlie, old man,' (this to his pal within), 'there's something doing on the Canal bank.' The others came out in a hurry, in time to see a line of vermilion lights soaring or sinking over the Hun line about three miles south of us, and around these a prodigious interplay of spluttering white flares. Even to my unskilled eye these were birds of ill omen, and the trouble flamed up astonishingly quickly. Artillery began to low like bullocks and a crop of crimson fire-balls began to make their appearance – and disappearance – with muffled clangs around the danger spot. Shrapnel, I learned. At the same time, puzzling red sparks proceeded to crawl up from the Boche line, climb to their zenith and topple down into the British trenches, where they ended in a momentary blaze of light followed by a crunching roar – trench mortars. Meanwhile, a furious and unintermitted crackling had told of machine guns and rifles lending their effects, and mushroom lights of many colours shouldered up through the storm, hung a few seconds mocking and mowing over the smoke, and dropped burning. The noise of shrapnel was nearly incessant, but every minute a terrific 'Crrrump' belittled the other pandemonium. It was not so far away, I considered, after all. God save us (so early had my love for my new battalion taken root) from being shifted to Givenchy or wherever this alarming war scene was staged. There seemed no possible chance for the men huddling behind parapets or blundering up communication trenches in such a wholesale tornado. Thus I mused, fortunately for myself unable to read coming events, though sinister forebodings were marked in the tones of my companions. Hardened warriors as these were in comparison with me, they were evidently impressed by this splenetic and pyrotechnic concerto. 'I say, a bit thick isn't it?' ... 'Hope to God we don't get pushed down the other side of the Canal' ... 'You bet your boots we shall' ... 'Whose is it, ours or theirs?' ... 'Looks as if we're doing a raid' ... 'By gad they are chucking rum-jars about' ... 'Jehosh! I'll bet you that was a mine' ... 'Our gunners are slamming it over like hell now' ... 'Comic Cuts will have some fruity paras. tomorrow' ... 'Seems to be slacking off a bit' ... 'Yes, Boche isn't gunning at all now' ... 'Well, I'm off in for a whisky – coming? MESS!'

The affair having wearied itself out, the night gradually resolved itself into odd shots and bursts of fire, distant clatter of transport, nervous Very lights, and the clink of shovels and indistinct blasphemies that betray a working party. L— led the way through the trench, which he referred to as the Old British Line, or (condensed) OBL. In the blackness it appeared a most formidable earthwork, rivalling the photos I had seen of the Great Wall of China; but L— (not that I believed him) said that 'it wouldn't stop a bullet, much less a whizzbang.' The sentries, too, gazing intrepidly over the top with bayonets fixed, struck me as Homeric – more of those 'strong, silent men': and it was with disappointment that I discovered they were in a kind of oblivion to everything except the approach of the next relief. They had 'heard some firing' down at Givenchy! I noticed that they one and all wore cap comforters, from which I gathered that there was an order forbidding these soporifics: and so it proved to be. The romance of war was being somewhat simplified for me, and I now took the opportunity of asking L— to explain certain abracadabra which appeared to be part of the fighting man's outfit.

With much less scorn than I had presaged he expounded: 'Comic Cuts, that's a huge mass of paper the Intelligence nuts send round every day, all about crumps, pumps and dumps: you'll see it tomorrow. That show was down on the Canal – the canal from Béthune to La Bassée – but for God's sake don't talk about that place because we'll see enough of it according to The General. Look, there's a rum-jar going over – see the sparks! They've got some trench mortars down there weighing about a couple of hundredweight – some mild rebuff if they catch you on the tin hat. You'll get a tin hat presently: some people wear them! But this is about the cushiest part of the line. Well, old thing, we might as well be getting back home.' Home! Six feet by six, with every modern discomfort; hardly rain-proof, but (by a kindred fallacy with that of the hunted ostrich) accredited shelter from all Teutonic malice; fuggy, draughty withal, rat-stricken, primeval, crampt, and crowded, yet housing (as I soon recognised) stout hearts, good cheer, and unhesitating friendliness. So home we

went to the dugout, with no other incident than the occasional mosquito-whine of a bullet spinning askew off the
barbed wire, and the unwieldy scuttling of wheezy rats in
the sudden unnerving glare of the Very Lights. It seemed a
time, times and a half since I left England. I crawled into
the sandbag bed and joined the chorus of gentle snores.

# CHAPTER 3
## 'First Depressions'

A sandbag bed is easily prepared. Your batman is the Merlin of the case, unless he has for the time effaced himself on some errand ostensibly connected with the Mess. His recipe is, to 'win' fifty sandbags or thereabouts, which he will do if there are but fifty-one on the dump. *Deus ex machina* he reappears in the dugout and arranges the spoils mattress-fashion in a corner, or recess. Professional touches are added: one, a blanket of sandbags tied together; two, a sandbag stuffed with other bags to do duty as pillow. Such a bed is not surpassed by the Shelleian shakedown of roses or similar blooms, nor by the ancestral feather-bed and hop-pillow with which your farmhouse aunt always dignifies you at Christmas. At least, it seemed so in those days of easy contentment and sandbags innumerable. There was a kindly smell of linseed oil about new bales of sandbags which alone wove a drowsiness round me, and in proportion as the work had been stiff the sleep was sweet. Minor troubles one must admit there were; barring good luck or judgement, one began to freeze from the feet upwards in the small hours (except in high summer); and as the sandbags were apt to moult in tiny wisps, breathing was a little hairy. But the wise man always cased his legs in two or three sandbags, one inside the other; spread his towel beneath his head; and shrouded him (first layer) with his British Warm.

My first night's rest in the trenches, albeit not ensured with such scientific care, was perfect, and unhaunted even on its farthest verge by dream or fantasque. At last I heard voices and breakfast clatter, and through the doorway the sunlight was splendid, on bleaching unfamiliar sandbags.

Shock-headed and gaping I evolved from my lair, and was greeted with slight laughter. Ten o'clock! ... 'You don't mean to say you've got up!' ... 'I thought you had begun to get down to it' ... 'Not so bad as old Boz; he's good for another few hours' ... 'Don't you worry, boy: you take all the rest you can. They'll wake you up fast enough if they want you.' Soon afterwards the obese batman aforesaid brought me a biscuit-tin full of water, and in due course I was clean, in my right mind, and (like the Sunday paper's felon awaiting execution) 'eating a hearty breakfast'. L—, who was more commonly called Boz, had not yet slept his sleep, but was presently the victim of a minor enterprise and haled blinking and peevish into the light of day. The Company Commander now ordained that he was to chaperone me again round the company trenches and further display the seamy side of war, particularly the duties of the Officer on Watch (my name having been added to the list of employees). At this I was greatly pleased, having secretly resolved the night before to fill in this appalling abyss in my general knowledge from L—'s hoard of experience so kindly thrown open. (I am not sure that he was equally pleased, as he had fixed with a kindred spirit to thrid the fascinating ruins of Festubert that morning.)

We drifted idly out and along the trench, where boots protruding beneath sackcloth dugout doors gave L— his cue to 'hoik out' the unwary scrimshankers and set them on sundry trench repairs. The hot gold sun was already drowsy in the blue, and the war seemed to have slunk into a corner and fallen asleep. Old friends seemed to be all round; a skylark was floating and climbing steep above us, like his cousins over Sussex lands, with his fine melody let fall in prodigal enchantments. There was the growing drone of summer in the grassfields and orchards behind, and on the broken hawthorn tree the blackbird was asking what war was; and did not see the sparrowhawk hanging bloodthirstily over the stubbles. A tabby cat came sleekly round a traverse and purred peace and goodwill. My own idea of war improved wonderfully, till presently a sickly

breeze came by with history of the great and murderous
battle here a year ago, and L— pointed me out the skulls,
jagging bones, and wooden crosses with their weather-
worn 'TO AN UNKNOWN BRITISH SOLDIER' and
'R.I.P.', on the side of the trench. Of these there was no
lack, and out in the open L— said there were still unburied
skeletons in rotted uniforms. These wooden crosses, gaunt,
cynical, earthy, seemed utterly unfriendly to the momentary peace and beauty, or perhaps somewhat akin to the
poems of Homer; the forlorn memorials of some far-off
tribal bloodshed and horror not to be encountered again.
And yet – 'KILLED IN ACTION: MAY 9th, 1915.' But I
felt sure that this style of war was utterly obsolete. This was
another case of ignorance and bliss.

We were regarding a metal curio installed in its own
niche in the parapet, and stated by L— to be a 'Vermoral
Sprayer' for nullifying gas (after the manner of hop-
washing), when a sound such as the fanning wings of a
prize roc might make hirpled overhead, changed into a
whizz and was followed by a cloud of raddled dust and
black smoke and a roar in an outhouse some three hundred
paces behind us. More came swooping invisibly and idly
over and slipped with a kind of skidding noise into the
evanescent hut. The convulsed remains leapt in renewed
tortures. Instinct at once enlightened me that this was
shelling, but added that it was far enough away to be worth
watching. L— however, after the first visitation, betrayed a
want of enthusiasm and presently imparted the icono-
clasm. 'If he drops a short, it'll most likely land just about
where we're standing. You never know what the swine's
going to do. Let's get on a bit.' My zeal deflated and I trod
on his heels. The shells soon stopped; the building had
finished its useful career; the Hun had fired his morning
ration of offensiveness, and all parties were satisfied.

My impression of the trench (we were in the comfort of
reserve positions) was now condensing into a glorified ditch
between two sandbag banks, lined with groups of sentries;
gloomy alcoves inscribed with witty names; lazar-holes

crammed with bomb boxes or ammunition; graves, lime, old bayonets, braziers; and the saving grace of indolence over all. We passed one group of men scouring the already spotless components of a Lewis Gun; others employed on such artistic work as polishing eighteen-pounder cases dangling for use as tomtoms in a gas alarm, or collecting match-stalks from under the duckboards; others again assembled round a mound behind the trench from which they were evicting rats with assistance from a sand-coloured mongrel and yet others pleasingly engrossed in that necessary pursuit known as 'chatting', with the perpetual epithets applied to these minor enemies. Duck-boards, officially 'trench gratings', which name was doomed from birth, were laid along the trench bottom all the way; and in some of the fire-bays bags marked RUBBISH in indelible pencil (one of the chief factors in BEF) explained the drawing-room condition of this war-scene. A sooty dungeon of corrugated iron, exhaling smoke at numerous crevices and tenanted by two of the blackest and greasiest knaves in France, proved to be the cookhouse; in other words, the headstone of the corner. Dinner in two courses, first a complication of bully beef and onions, next a 'biscuit duff', was under way. Here the gloom of igno-rance was dispelled for me by the good offices of L—. The General, it appeared, had willed that the soldiers should be largely nurtured on duff, fig, currant, date or otherwise; and even went so far in this unnatural desire as to have duff served at his own table, to the distress of epicures like the Staff Captain. Imitation dog biscuits, he went on, were sent up on the ASC most days to the curtailment of the bread ration; these were pounded up with deplorable ingenuity into flour and (as now) converted into duff. If cross-examined by the General, 'Do you know what your men are having for dinner?' I was invariably to mention duff. From this L— digressed into the thorny paths of Whims and Oddities of the General, introducing a new unpleasant uncertainty into my imagined Arcadia, and that the worst of all so far. Not so much the General's likes and dislikes in detail depressed me; but the fact that there was a General at all. Previously, his existence here in the trenches had not flitted (a bat-like shadow) across my mind. Now, I should be awake of nights! Meanwhile, we had come to the right-hand limit of our line, where there happened to be a small but terribly permanent-looking machine-gun emplace-ment of brick, iron and concrete. Evidently the war was officially expected to last out a generation or two, and my horizon grew blacker still.

We now turned back and discovered that, whatever display of energy had been in train before, everyone save the sentries and cooks had been spirited away. The time of day grew sultrier and a blue haze swam on the distant country, which here I stood up on the fire-step to look upon: a flat marshy lowland, overgrown with tall dry grass, scarred and murrainous with trenches old and new, inter-sected with dead straight roads. Behind the zone of bombardments there were avenues of poplars, and several country houses not much dismembered: in the zone, there were occasional walls breast-high and tall trees along the roads struck in two by shells; other trees, save the few orchard-trees in the pale of etiolated farmhouses, and oziers on the dykes, there did not seem to be. A far-off gun had been firing for a moment or two and now insisted on our noticing it – as L— did by calling 'There's a Fritz up somewhere – hear that Archie. Look, they're shooting right up above us.' There they were, dozens of white shrapnel-spores and more following; and how Lilliputian seemed their diminished reports. Among these swiftly dispersed snowflakes drifting on the light breeze there was a flash, and a twinkling silver atom, flying westwards as if pursued by the foul fiend, drove across the blue. 'There goes Fritz,' stammered L— with heavenward finger. 'I expect it's one of their scouts going back to photograph Béthune.' He almost suffocated with wrath against our Archies whose shots were now about half a mile off the plane. 'What absolute waste. They've fired off over a hundred rounds, all for nothing: why the hell don't they join the Salvation

Army? Half a quid a time – that's fifty quid gone west in ten minutes, a damned scandal.' His bile was not lessened by the fact that now a venomous buzzing began, and among its many notes one suddenly whirred into fortissimo and a splinter of steel landed whack on the sandbags beside his head. This meteoric obnoxiousness (which should have led to a delightful letter from Gilbert White) quickened our return to the dugout.

A good dinner was the next 'feat of arms' as L— put it. He also wished the Company Commander formally to present me with the Freedom of the Burrow, but withdrew this on the arrival of a runner with various papers, including the renowned 'Comic Cuts'. This hardly came up to my expectations, although the mention of a place called Salome raised a crop of witticisms. The main idea of the author appeared to be to detect 'Water thrown over the parapet at Z25 d. 09.47', 'Smoke from suspected cook-house about Z24 a. central', and other incontestable proofs that the enemy daily washed and fed himself. Censoring letters and writing my own kept me busy from now almost till dark; and then I had nothing to do (except take my turn on watch), and spent the time reading poems and thinking things over. The sound sense of what I had seen in this short time, the chances of excitement, the 'return to nature' feeling, and the goodwill of everyone, made a great appeal to me: but on this sunlit mental sward descended two Cacodaemons brandishing monstrous clubs, the Possible Intrusion of catechising Generals, and the Probable Duration of the War.

# CHAPTER 4
## *Drowsed with the Fume of Poppies*

These placid early summer days, just kept alive by stray shots and new impressions, not wholly devoid of flowers and native woodnotes, leisurely and well-liking to a degree of luxury, were to become my regretful dream a few months later. Their exact history has been lost to me in the crowded times between, but still I see myself at many a spot from Neuve Chapelle to Cuinchy Brickstacks, a humble Don Quixote facing war with beautiful idiocy. Taking the lackadaisical disturbances of our life behind breastworks and under sheets of corrugated iron for the full-blown violence of war, I worked earnestly and thought nothing trivial. Ruined hen-houses and rusted harrows spelt pathos and romance, a duty such as visiting 'posts' in the mists and fusillade of morning stand-to demanded steeling of nerves and seemed an adventure. Thus, the first really uncomfortable episode – a scramble to the front line overland, in pallid, whimsical moonlight – is still vivid to me; whilst fifty worse jobs later on are out of mind. This midnight gavotte 'Thoro' mud, thoro' wire', showed my eyes (eagerly dilated) the Old German Line of 1915. It lay mute and inglorious across our path, a great ditch torn with ancient gunfire, still held by its unconquerable dead. In the false light all things looked terrible; but there was one sufficiently gruesome, the bones of a German still pinned to the ground by the unexploded shell that had hit him. A sudden stream of bullets moved us on from this gallery of disaster. Filled with a wild idea that we should shortly blunder into the new German line, I was glad when (after imaginary hours of walking) we ceased to stumble into shell-holes, petrol cans and festoons of wire, and struck a duckboard track. And at last through a sort of sand-bag postern we arrived in the front trench.

Here there was a State of War, men firing rifles and now and then even the Lewis gunners 'keepin' Fritz's 'ead down'. The officer on trench patrol proved to be an old acquaintance, and patiently explained the position to me; a few bony trees in front were Canadian Orchard, of which he seemed rather nervous. 'I'll just put up a Very light old man,' he grunted, brandishing a sort of brass cannon and putting in a cartridge. 'Stop your ears, the old duck-gun wakes the dead.' A murderous bang, a spluttering flame flying up, then a few gloomy red sparks, and 'as you were'. At the sixth attempt a flare soared with some vigour, died in air and dropped; then by way of answer, sneering, calm and dazzling, three or four rose from the Boche lines and fell sizzling and white-hot in the grass behind our lines: sentries ducked along the silhouetted parapet, which was promptly flayed with machine-gun bullets. At that time our flares were so poor that the Germans would sometimes throw up lighted matches from their trench in mockery. There was even an idle fiction, but widely believed, rewarding the fortunate man who captured a German *licht-patron* with a fortnight's leave. And shortly after this, it became a point of honour in the battalion to fire no lights at all unless the Hun was at the gate.

Going into the company headquarters I found my contemporary D——, rubbing his eyes and shaking off odd sandbags. His Irish nature had no fault to find with this small smoke-dried cabin; except when a bullet plopped into the wall just by his head. This was evidence of the discomforts of a salient. 'An enemy hath done this,' remarked D—— and refilled his glass. But it would soon be getting light now, so the visitors departed the way they had come, and had hardly jumped into the Old British Line when the early twittering of larks and crescendo of rifle-shots, in their different fashions, welcomed the dawn.

Soon after this the company took over what were known as 'stand-to' billets in the ill-balanced brickwork of Festubert. The actual move was perhaps five hundred yards, but the prospect of meddling with semi-destruction or evolving a pleasant melancholy among some deserted currant-bushes, perhaps even finding a book in the château cellar, aroused my zeal. We marched quietly in, one pitchy night, passing the infamous Brewery Corner with appropriate awe; and the men were settled in sandbagged ruins and holes proudly called 'keeps'. Soup was to be got at the Aid Post, and it was there I first made the acquaintance of the strong silent man who was to be my henchman, pioneer, steward, patrol assistant, in a word *Batman*, for somewhat over two years. His first office was to shepherd me to the officers' dugout, a sort of sandbagged steel tunnel, under the name of a 'big elephant', built inside an undesirable detached villa. Next morning I took the air and spied out the land, in brilliant sunshine, so much so that there was a slight influx of war-workers varying from whizzbangs to woolly bears. In the intervals, however, I snatched a fearful joy, and gathered in a small sheaf of idle straws betraying the barrenness of war – odd side-lights – tailpieces to the bitter ever-astonishing epic. My letters tried to be anything but diaries, and so were full of gardens unkempt and shrines disgodded, relics of peace and even of the early war. In this way my view of Festubert was somewhat out of focus; and while I had no palest glimmering of its pros and cons as a strong point in event of a Boche break-through, indeed did not connect it with the remote firing-line – a mile distant, – yet I could have led you by night blindfold to the biggest Johnson 'Ole, loneliest wooden cross, or least battered cottage in the place. The village was fairly occupied with our own guns, but I only knew the position of the battery nearest our dugout, and then only because it was masked with pleasant cunning in a wall. Whenever the gunners felt like a few rounds, a part of the brickwork would betray itself and slide back; the firing finished, the gap would close again, and the wall resume its role of love and charity.

My duties in this period were, mainly, going round the company at 'stand-to', at daybreak and at dusk; taking

pick-and-shovel troops forward to dig communication
trenches by night; censoring letters; and aiding and abet-
ting K—, the art-worshipper among us, to sing 'Great Tom
is cast'. Altogether he taught L— and myself five rounds,
whose maltreated melody must still haunt the tortured ruin
where we sung. K— was a clever artist and adorned the
walls with two charcoal drawings of great immodesty and
wittiness. His conversation was amazing, a sort of mental
acrobatics. I was a good listener to the free and freakish
palavering with which the brothers-in-arms transformed
the chlorinated water and camouflaged bully of our meals
into very banquets. Once my ears tingled at an account of
recent fighting at Vimy, where the shellfire had been such
(said our gossip), that the British lines were exactly like a
ploughed field, and further a Fusilier battalion had come
out of the trenches with its strongest company totalling 1
officer and 16 men. This was too much for my imagination.
I put it down to the Quartermaster's Stores (the source of
so much picturesque romance) and like the deaf adder
stopt my ears. My notebook, refusing hearsay, was eloquent
on such more accessible ferocities as the 'crump-hole in the
garden, 25 feet across and 8 deep' – 'tumid rumours of Gas
last night but nothing happened, and thank God' – 'village
school smashed and three men's rifles blown up by heavy
shelling' – 'on working party again: I thought to pass away,
yet here alive I am' – 'passed Crucifix outside shattered
Church at 2 this morning and thought it was a ghost until
I heard a bullet hit it' – 'watched some obese rats turn cart-
wheels when our big gun loosed off just behind them'. I was
specially proud to record taking a cold bath one sunny
morning, in this heroic village which must have been one
of the finest rest-cures on the front. Again and again do its
broken laths and glimmering shrine loom up in my recall;
the heavy dew and ricochets and blackbird-flutes of early
morning; the incredible tom-tom croaking of innumerable
frogs in the dikes and culverts; the indolent midday under
runaway flowering boughs; the evening tramp up communication trenches – full of the 'dead man smell' of that

marshland, suggesting a ferment of Church lilies; and
starry midnight dreaming a majesty on those humble lath-
and-plaster ruins, the whooping owls by the Church corner,
the groaning stretcher-cases borne along the street, past my
fairy rosebush blossomed silverly beyond belief; all these
things and many more still make Festubert for me what it
was then, 'a tale, a dream', the village beyond the world.
There I truly enjoyed the war, and touched new mentality.

Meanwhile, I was beginning to know and be known in
the Company, though terrified of nearly everyone outside
it, whether General or Serjeant-Major. I well remember
the concerned expressions of two officers, later on well-
known to me, to whose dugout I was sent on some duty
which compelled me to wait there. 'Have a drink?' 'No
thanks, I don't drink.' 'Have a cigarette?' 'No thanks, I
don't smoke.' 'Play bridge?' 'Sorry, I don't play cards.'
'Well, what the hell *do* you do?' No known heading apparently applied to me. Nevertheless, my knowledge of Sussex
appealed to the men, as also my efforts on their behalf to
persuade vacant RE officers of the merits of Piece Work.
This zeal often saw us finish a job in two or three hours and
file down the trench for 'home', where the plan of four
hours' digging would have meant finicky work and ill
temper. Sometimes I would come from these working
parties the sadder and quieter for a casualty or two: and
Death is so whimsical in war that we have in 'quiet sectors'
lost perhaps a dozen men by occasional sniping or wild
firing, whereas in a morass of still-multiplying shell-holes
and under daily and nightly barrages we have escaped with
less mortality.

From our fragmentary village street we next moved
forward to the front line, where we fossilised by day and
feared the General by night for about a week. Even to my
easily contented eye, the British defences here seemed
rather parlous, albeit sited in a quagmire. A front line
trench there had apparently been, but the winter had
flooded it out and only here and there had previous tenants
been able to keep their heads above water – some were

drowned – by continual sandbagging. Now the warmer weather was beginning to dry the clay, and our position was a cordon of 'islands' more or less arising from a shallow impassable ditch while a short way behind these were snatches of breastwork by way of mainstays. Why the observant Boche did not clean up these impudent sandbag swindles one morning before breakfast has often seemed a puzzle since, but he respected their threadbare and invalid look, and, while he might have 'minnied' or gunned us out in a few light-hearted rounds, contented himself with sniping and amusements at 'stand-to'. Two machine-guns of his were not so charitable and earned nicknames – Blighty Albert, and Quinque Jimmy. Their crews seemed to be warned by diabolic agency whenever our ration parties or like unfortunates were sweating under their nightly burdens on Quinque Rue. The two guns would open up as one and cross fire, mostly allying with the Very-light man; then the sparks would flick and the lead richochet off the cat's-head camber, and several figures would flop in the ditch breathing fire and slaughter against the 'blarsted bastards', until the tyranny was overpast. Small wonder that the bread ration sometimes arrived, like the bacon, reinforced with wet sandbag and sugar.

One night, as L— and myself sat purring peace and goodwill in the ramshackle lean-to already described, the inevitable happened – hurried voices without: *pomposo*, 'Where is your Company Headquarters my man?' … *patetico alla con moto*, ''Ere you are sir' … *staff captaino*, 'Yaas thah it is sah' – enter two visions in crimson and gold, gas masks on breasts. The General! and rampant. He treated L— with some brusqueness, betraying a feud of some standing over the question of 'inspecting wire', then registered on me with such disastrous queries as 'Have you been round the wire?' and 'Well, why not?' At the close of the session (but he was the only one sitting) he had scored heavily, and L— and myself were left 'to face the naked days' in horrid apprehensions, and amid unpleasant duties. We made the best of them, inspecting the wire with scientific zeal, locating our Lewis Guns, even knowing 'what our men had had for breakfast' and 'why no porridge' each morning.

A week soon slipped past. Each day was only the counterpart of dreamy yesterday; the batmen would be 'missing' save for meals from dawn till dewy eve, dozing sweetly (permit the conjecture) in the long grass behind the trench; the flies would bask on the baking sandbags; the grasshoppers crick all round as in an English homefield, and many a mouse squeak unmolested over the crumbs of parcels from home. The German sharpshooters might fire once or twice in the afternoon, but only at *bona-fide* marks: the ferocious plaster heads which our sentries might in ebullient moments hoist ever so gingerly, surveyed the scenery without let or hindrance from them. A covey of whizzbangs hurtled over us one morning scarcely regarded, which, nevertheless, nearly spoiled the Colonel and Major as they were emerging from their sanctum in the OBL behind. Our own dugout was respected despite the tumid smokestack insolently fuming from the 'kitchen'; and as yet I had no cause to regret the Minnie, the Oilcan, the Pineapple and the Woolly Bear. These were to come, in liberal education. Our days, unsmirched with Hun baseness, were equally void of visiting critics from Brigade and Division; the communication trench was not working, and we were marooned. After dark, however, machine-guns, mosquitoes, mandarins, and musketeers bustled into life and labour; with clink and twang the wirers fumbled out in front, and in front of them with mixed feelings the patrollers ferretted through the wet grass. The General was wont to collate every morning the Wire Reports of his various battalions and companies, as set out on one of his celebrated Pro Formas: a kind of Score Sheet it was, indicating 'Place of Work, Time, Officer, No. of Men, No. of Yards Put Up, No. of Coils, (*a*) Barbed, (*b*) Concertina; No. of Pickets, (*a*) Wood, (*b*) Iron', and probably other statistics. The essential was, good round numbers in the 'No. of Coils' column: woe worth that Company Commander who claimed the lowest figure in the Brigade for a night's work! Few would risk this, but deceit was out of the question. Colossal numbers were reported, and the General placated. There has always been a tale, however, doubtless started and manoeuvred by coarse cynics in our two rival brigades, that the coils put out by us were dumped bodily in the mud – and even that Fritz, noticing a few dozen in one place, came over and removed them for his own use. Honni soit! At all events, our object was achieved, and the General's breakfast thirst for statistics slaked without dishonesty.

Every night patrols went out. K— was the noted sleuth; but one morning as he groped round a ruin accused of being a sniper's post, daylight surprised him and in the handicap back to our lines two of his party were hit. He wrote a vivid account of his night's work, which the General, thinking fondly of his own stereotyped reports, found 'too "flowery"'.

[Note the quotation marks round 'flowery'. The militarist mind never yet hit on a word of vigour or expressiveness without so apologising for its use. I suppose dignity would be at stake if a dud were not termed a 'dud' (or rather, a 'blind' shell), a dropped round 'dropped', and so on. The Army Pamphleteer must be sparing of such words even with their nakedness veiled; let him play the illiterate Johnson and evolve a sort of bastard Latin; for so doing he shall save his soul alive. I have at hand a memorandum from an Author already quoted, dating from those Festubert times. Its majestic march and 'deliberate instancy' begin thus: –

## THE ORGANISATION OF DUTIES IN A BATTALION AND ITS COMPANIES

1. The separation of duties connected with Operations and training from duties connected with Interior Economy and Administration.

Whether in the Trenches, in Billets, in Camp or in

Barracks it is impossible to carry out military duties effi-
ciently or conveniently without good organisation. Good
organisation lies in the sub-division and distribution of
duties and in the delegation of responsibility to a
number of persons, while at the same time retaining in
one hand guidance and control, so as to ensure unifor-
mity of methods and adherance to a well considered and
clearly defined system or plan.

'And there was light!' But to return, only in imagination,
to the trenches.]

As to my own nightly exploits, I took things very seriously. One night while, guided by my batman, I was visiting
the 'islands', we were suddenly the object of quite a fusillade. Why this well-aimed hate against two poor souls?
Could the German eye pierce the cloud of night? – no, the
cheap and nasty electric torch in my pocket had somehow
turned itself on, and Fritz was merely following the gleam.
This grim episode was the worst of the week; but our existence and abode savoured so much of imprisonment for life
that I rejoiced to hear one hot afternoon the metallic but
timely voice of the Company Commander: 'We're going
back to Hinges tomorrow, I want you to go down first thing
in the morning and take over billets.'

# CHAPTER 5
## *Uncertainty of Life*

Six o'clock and a pleasant morning. I had come down to the Old British Line during the night, and, seeking rest in the reserve company headquarters, had been unlucky. The only place vacant in the dugout was a form, where I balanced with difficulty, swathed in an overcoat. At the hour aforesaid, the Company Commander awoke – he had been asleep when I arrived – and believing me to be still dreaming drawled out 'What's that thing?' I supplied the information, decided that the little sleep I had had was all I should get, and left. (Later in the year I was enabled to see the blasé one in other moods.) Presently I found the other officers of the billeting party, and meekly followed them through an orchard complete with cemetery, barricades of broken tumbrils and barrels, and dud shells piously enclosed in barbed wire, on to a trolley-line through fields of untilled luxuriance. We passed some of the early attempts at digging in, which once more suggested how long the war could be expected to last considering how long it had lasted already, and the present monotony. Nature at least seemed to approve of it in this district; small lizards slid from their sunbath into their dugouts as we passed; the self-sown wheat was swarming with small birds, hares, and wild-flowers; and not a ditch but was in a flurry with tiny fish such as Walton called skipjacks. The time passed quickly for me noticing these things until we reached the railhead on a pavé road, close to a farmstead smoking genially to heaven – the REs were preparing dinner! It was a few hundred yards along this road that we met an officer on horseback, who stopped to talk; he was to play a great part in the battalion's drama presently, as its finest CO. But at this time I saw in him only another daily danger.

We sweated along, now, into a region of estaminets, beet fields and farm carts – and I should add, staff cars. As a proof of our preparedness for all possibilities, even here were belts of barbed wire and positions for machine-guns, no less than five miles behind our front! My surprise, in the light of after-experience, was not unreasonable. At last our dusty drudgery ended, and, arriving at the company head-quarters assigned to us I made myself known to the Cambridgeshire officers there and was received most pleas-antly. The company was to be billetted in two farms of almost identical shape, size and smell; the mess, however, was clean and cool; we were perhaps lucky to be near the canal and within sound and shadow of many poplar trees. The business of prowling round in the guise of a sanitary inspector and surveyor took up the afternoon: I signed without qualms for a variety of things, having a sort of instinct that, no matter how spotless the billets were, some lynx would bring to notice an uncollected Woodbine packet or a derelict tooth-brush next day. The Cambridgeshires presently moved out coated with the parcels from home which always arrive on the day of a move; and after midnight I met C company and ushered them in under a sharp fire of questions. The last thing before the officers went to bed, a runner from the orderly room brought in a document which pleased nobody. It was a Training Programme, apparently the work of diabolical agency, but signed by the Adjutant. I began to wish for the rat-run ease of the front line again. L— wished likewise. Our views were generally at one, and he was of all my new acquaintance, the one who scared me least.

Daylight was creeping on when I got to bed – and my batman arrived to pull me from the luxury of sheets at two in the afternoon: it had been raining and the dust was laid, even unto mud. This was 'cleaning-up' day, and I found the Troops – their own phrase – already improving the Shining Hour: not only shining, but scrubbing and sweeping, too. A new Company Commander had taken charge – a Major;

and similarly his servant had assumed control of the Mess. This Major was in many ways an astonishing man, although regarded askance by some of the men. An aristo, features and gestures announced him – a virtuoso with various arts at his fingertips, but more a man of attainments than of gifts – a vegetarian who natheless tackled his rasher for breakfast – a sort of lesser Byron by descent and ambition – finally, a past master in conversation, and yet possessing more wit than wisdom. He used epigram like a rapier. I once or twice got him to discuss poetry, and understood the brilliant but minor verse of his father better after hearing his tastes. His delicate but sometimes wounding speech, coupled with his luxurious living and extravagant expression of disgust even at the lesser discomforts of the trenches, hardly made him popular with the long-suffering rank and file. Such was the new arrival in our company mess. The day was soon spent in inspections, paying out (5 francs a man, munition workers –) and trial of malefactors. I was finding out that the fact of a man's being on active service was no safeguard from trivial quiffs, eyewash, and officiality, details of which will crop up in my account of trench matters a little later. That evening after dinner – we lived fatly at that time – I passed through the kitchen of the French people, and was induced to take a seat and a 'Café M'sieu?' There were an unknown number of inmates; they kept appearing like fish in a weedbed; but the chief figures were the *père* still wearing his railway-man's cap with patent leather brink, and Marie aged twenty-odd keeping house. *Maman* was not mentioned. The old man chumped away at his buff-hued bread, and gurgled pensively over a sort of vegetable soup – remarks in patois passed among the family – my claim to be nineteen years of age was received with surprise. Before the evening finished, this weather-bitten old peasant had recited, and accompanied with appreciations, a couple of La Fontaine's fables for my benefit.

The following morning was a trial for me. The Training Programme ordained Platoon Drill, an art which was not my main object in life. The major who had first come into my sphere on the way down from the line made his second appearance, and my nervousness increased to a terrible degree. He hardly knew whether to be angry or sorry for me. My deliverance was sudden, owing to the advent of the Colonel. The company was formed up round him, to my surprise, and then he commenced a harangue. It appeared that one of the men had been stiffly punished for some 'crime', and that a number of his pals had – against every precept and ordinance of the Regular Army – addressed a round robin of complaint to the Adjutant. (On hearing of this enormity my ears tingled, and I forgot that men ten miles off were indulging in war! No, somehow I couldn't detect quite wherein the enormity lay, in respect to the civilian army of 1914.) Whatever punishment the offender had got, the CO proceeded, this kicking over the traces was a most serious breach of discipline, and a disgrace to the regiment. He intended to drop very heavily on any repetition of it ... By this time beads of perspiration were standing out on a hundred brows; all felt their guiltiness – I was thus imagining a press version of the scene when the CO finished on the word 'ringleaders' and rode out of the field. In the afternoon we marched to baths; and then when we returned I had to answer the expected calumny as to taking over dirty billets – there are NCOs who make such complaints with an eye to attracting attention. Censoring and a kit inspection after tea brought me to the End of a Perfect Day. I 'got down to it' that night with the comforting knowledge that I was to be orderly officer tomorrow.

And so I was. A pair of kid gloves were unearthed for me, and the orderly serjeant was a member of my platoon. The Adjutant was away on some special duty, so I made my rounds without too much knocking at the knees; and, keeping my eyes open, made some useful mental notes on what was usual in the battalion. About tea-time all officers were called to headquarters, no one knew why, until we were haled inside. The Adjutant, wearing if anything a more saturnine aspect than ever, stated in ban-dog tones that 'there was something in the air', and we should have to be ready for a move forward at an hour's notice. This was perhaps not such bad news, if every time we came out of the trenches we were to be subject to Training Programme. As we came out of the conference (war hath his conferences too), someone said, 'I knew we'd be tooling up the road again when we'd just come out to rest.'

For my part, the return was not yet; the company marched off, but I was left to attend a gas course at Essars, three miles off. This gave me three pleasant days unmolested. My batman kept house for both of us, in the so soon deserted Mess. I used to walk to and fro every day, along the canal and by narrow paths through the cornfields; content if I happened to catch sight of a shoal of roach in the water or anything else that spoke of peace. Béthune, whither all the other officers on the course scurried off every evening, was so far no attraction to me. Essars itself was intact, and the petty shopkeepers there would be able to retire comfortably enough, unless the course of the war changed, within a year or two. Never was there such a roaring trade in trash, such a display of eye-withering silk cards and rosaries, vile violet pencils and sweltering chocolate. As to the gas course, it was excellent – a young Welsh officer was in charge, who really had got his subject under his hand and spoke good English. What other courses I have undergone in the army have been endeavours to turn axioms into sciences, and to darken knowledge with jargon. What methods and weapons were actually in use in the line, the instructors pooh-poohed, and proceeded to put before the bored classes the very finest eyewash, which would prove the right thing – on a drill ground! But this brief account and experience of gas was simplicity itself, and I never afterwards saw its organisers without admiration.

The morning soon came which found my batman and me plodding with our belongings on our backs in murderous heat along the towpath. Where the battalion were now was a riddle, but anyway we were going to find them. The evening before they had been at Le Quesnoy, which I found was somewhere between Béthune and the

trenches. I asked a Frenchman about it, in Béthune. He
with the quick perception of his race hastened to inform
me that Le Q. was now in the hands of the Boche. I
explained that I wanted another place of that name. He
somehow took this as discourtesy and with a shrug and a
scowl made off. However, we presently reached the hamlet
of Le Quesnoy by way of the canal bank, and were
rewarded with news of the battalion – in the trenches at
Cuinchy. It had been sultry when we set out, but now as we
left the area of civilians and estaminets our packs weighed
tons. At the last surviving buvette we tried a revolting fluid
called GRENADIN FANTAISIE, which added to our
drouth. Towards Cuinchy village there was evidence of a
vigorous and quite recent war – shell-holes, telegraph wires
in hanks, rusty ruins of factories, gunpits, a forbidding lone-
liness, the canal like green glue, stagnant and stinking. The
effect of this surprising, unreal deformity, glowering
through the blue burning haze at the canal's seeming end,
was to make me feel like the victim of a trick. A control
sentry directed us down 'Harley Street' to our battalion
headquarters. The scarecrow houses leaned to watch us on
both sides, silent as the grave.

# CHAPTER 6

## *The Wrong Side of the Canal*

Abig building in fairly good shape housed battalion headquarters, but did not mark the close of our wanderings. A guide was aroused from his afternoon doze and led us by a zigzag of chalk trenches into a sort of support system, where under a few morsels of farm building we found the company dugout. From there we were once more moved on, and finally cast anchor in a shell-trap called Whizzbang Keep. Here I was pleased to find L— at table in a stuffy little black hole which, nevertheless, had been a real home from home that morning to its occupants. The Germans had put over about six hundred shells on the ruins above, which I had escaped. There was not much to do here except to scare off the flies and await events; but we were shortly relieved, and returned to company headquarters. This was quite a large dugout, which had started life as a cellar; the entrance was not much to look at but somehow bigger men than Little Tich went in and out by it. Of course candles had to be kept alight in this cavern all day, and the air was somewhat heavy, but in these respects it was true to the type, and also in its contents: bunk beds, purloined chairs and table, SOS rockets, loose bombs on a shelf, several jars of issue lime-juice, a volume of O. Henry, and unregarded tins of bully. The day following, I saw a more commodious dugout – it was the cellar of 'Kingsclere', where I had been set to draw maps by order of the Adjutant. Here BHQ lived in some comfort; there was air, and the light of day stole in at a lattice; a piano even, and a real bed occupied corners, and jars of garden flowers grown wild made quite a harmony of colour. But for these amenities I could see that nobody on headquarters had any leisure – too many URGENTs, SPECIALs, and PRESSINGs poured in from brigade. What I did not see was that the 'something in the air' spoken of by the Adjutant a few nights since was still hovering over us; although the place was full to a sophisticated eye of portents of trouble. I have since heard that a German attack was feared, but nothing of vast consequence actually occurred.

Life was certainly uneasy and violent half-hours were the rule; on our company area, for instance, there were several shoots. A deep trench lined with deep dugouts, Esperanto Terrace, was suddenly shrapnelled thirteen to the dozen one day at tea-time, and some of the men were caught by the first crash. The shells were mainly plump in the trench, and where I stood on the stairs of a dugout I had my first experience of hot blasts of air from shell-bursts just outside. Soon after this, as I was sleeping my time towards midnight, the dugout was apparently seized by an unknown hand and shoved seesaw fashion: everyone seemed to be calling out 'That's a Mine!' The company stood to arms, and I went outside, to be reminded of what I had seen, under more comfortable conditions, that night at Festubert. Once more 'there was something doing on the Canal Bank', whinings and cracklings and shatterings, mad echoes lumbering and racketing through the dark, gun-flashes and red shrapnel-spores and the death-dance of flares and rockets. Soon we were ordered by the Adjutant to send up a reinforcing platoon to the front line, where casualties had been heavy. This job fell to L— while I went up with a volunteer stretcher party. None of us knew the way, but we found where the wounded mostly were, after scrambling through the most awkward trenches and somehow dodging quite a deluge of five-nines. It was my first wild night. One of the wounded was in a very bad case, and over him hung his brother half frantic, himself wounded. Brothers in the same battalion – there were several pairs in this – give rise perhaps to the sharpest griefs of all in war. Meanwhile, L—'s men were digging out the dead and only just alive in the front line. In spite of the tremendous noise and confusion, the Germans made no infantry attack, and towards daybreak, the shelling died down.

After this episode I was pleased to be presented with a shrapnel helmet, which had been, with so many other desirable things, 'on indent'.

In the middle of the battle, the unfortunate Adjutant at 'Kingsclere' was trying to cope with the situation, and frantically canvassing front companies for news, by phone and runner. He was disturbed – a call from Brigade – perhaps there was urgent information from flank battalions? Perhaps not! At this critical moment his straining ear discerned the still small voice of the Staff Captain, solemnly pronouncing these relevant words: 'The Baths at Z 25 c 4.9 are allotted to you this morning' –

About this time magnificent rumours of a victory by the British fleet, and several dozen German ships scuppered, began to masquerade. A sound of cheering farther up the line was our first intimation. I once more began to think of the war as temporary. The same night came Pessimists, who substituted German for British and vice versa in the first bulletins. To this day, I don't know anything more definite about Jutland than I then did.

The company now moved into the front line. We were now proudly – but with chattering teeth – defending the ill-famed Brickstacks. Of all battle-fields this was perhaps the most grotesque and gripping. Brute, squat and monstrous, out of a flat wilderness queasy with gamboge darnel and festering heliotrope poppies, and waled with dirty white trench outlines, upstood a score or so of brickstacks. In the dim and distant past of the war, already almost traditional, these obvious forts had been fought for with a sort of mania; in the present impasse, the Germans and ourselves shared them almost equally, but far from equably. These maltreated masses of red brick covered a multitude of people and things. Each had its number, but one adjective did duty for all. Inside, stifling creepholes twisted up to

'secret' machine-guns and look-outs, with painted instruc-
tion-boards against the day of attack; below, muddy
staircases opened into tunnellers' and infantry's dugouts,
telephone centres and trench stores. From these nerve
centres with more or less effrontery led forward or backward a series of boyaux, alleys half choked with glutinous
pudder of a filthy grey, crumbling, aromatic, tangled with
signallers' wires. The front line itself was a mere ditch; with
defects. Of the German trenches our notion was a shadow;
though everyone knew that the carcase of a train on their
end of the railway hid a Teutonic sniper – a thing so likely
as to be unlikely.

An intolerable landscape, sickly yellow and sallow,
upheaved and brutalised, scrawled with leprous white, and
smutched with cinder-black – and, as though the bricks
were still burning, heat-fumes of blue shrouding the few
acres visible. Behind us cowered the rubble-heaps marked
Cuinchy on the map, but high over a communication
trench a white, beautiful calvary defied flying death. In
front, like the waste of dreadful days to come, stretched no-
man's-land, a blur, a curse to the eyes, gouged into great
craters and innumerable shell-holes, strewn with the appa-
ratus of wire entanglements.

One of these mine craters adorned wen-like our own
stretch of front line. Walking along the trench, one only saw
a sally-port cut under the sandbag parapet; slid down the
mud-chute thus indicated; and pulled up in a sort of
reversed crow's-nest at the bottom of a huge basin-pit.
Here, bate the breath – bob down and keep down – we are
winning but Boche mustn't know we think so; meanwhile,
the sentry stands watching with his periscope – we are officers – ready to shoot, the picture of vigilance. You feel like
Horatio? Want to tackle fifty Huns? This feeling results in
your peeping gingerly up, and – why, there's a Prussian
Guardsman (every time, the only German regiment) coolly
taking in the scenery from the far lip of the crater. Mind
yourself, his bomb's in the air; it splashes in the water
lodged at the bottom and with a muffled thunder spatters

everything with mud. Such was an average introduction to Jerusalem Crater.

A memorable message came down to company head-quarters from the Sussex cricketer C—, who happened to be the officer on trench duty. It ran, I think: – *Huns have just thrown 6 bombs into Jerusalem Crater. Shall we throw any back?*

The great defect of war here as elsewhere was the shortage of sleep; but I considered myself lucky to get any rest at all in this muckheap. The nightmare of hordes of Boches rampant never troubled me, still in the lap of igno-rant bliss, as I wandered from fire-bay to sap and sap to dump, waiting for the mists to clear and let the men stand down. Indeed, the barrack routine and discipline then prevailing in the front trenches might have convinced any newcomer that the war was a rumour. Every morning, however, gave the lie to this desirable notion; and I now had my first view of the Minnie, who appeared to be much fonder of the Brickstacks than we were. Her lair was cunningly sited in a pit which the gunners knew of but found most awkward even for the howitzers to disturb. The silence with which this minenwerfer fired from such a sanctum made us venture theories of electric guns and vanishing platforms. Whatever might be the method, the German minnie-man knew how to upset our domestic programme each morning, – sudden alarm, crouching and dodging; anxious eyes survey a small black devil wobbling over and over, high in the air; then down it shoots, people shout near the unlucky spot, the earth jolts and the air shat-ters. The puzzle of gauging where Minnie will drop is usually called sweating blood, and, the more Minnies in the air at once, the more frightful the blue sky and the jumping nerves. I remember reading in a dugout once a bantering article, of the usual *Punch* type, refined and donnish, entitled 'Trench Mortar Tennis'. I have long wanted, like Charles Lamb, to feel the author's bumps. He would no doubt trace a touching affinity between Salisbury Cathe-dral and the Folies-Bergères. At any rate, we never seemed to spot the wildly humorous side of a minenwerfer;

although my remark on my first experience of one, 'Good Lord, that's a big rifle grenade', awoke a pitying grin on the face of my platoon serjeant.

With depressing frequency, in the near or distant south, both sides blew mines and cavilled over them. One afternoon the sappers in our own sector displaced a few hundred tons of no-man's-land, on the shortest notice. The company stood to arms, the trench mortar officer appeared and disappeared, a tunneller talked with the company commander as to why and how, and all awaited the dirty minute in some pain. Four o'clock the monstrous hammer-blow down in the chalk rocked the ground and jarred the brain; and there stood in air a roaring fountain of black dust and piecemeal earth. Before a clod had toppled over again, in the pittering and chattering of jostling fragments, we had crowded the parapet flinging grenades and rattling away with Lewis guns, for no particular reason except noise and swashbuckling. The trench mortars and battalion bombers, with salvoes of Stokes and Newton Pippins, were dissuading the enemy from occupying the new crater; and there were evident signs that the enemy was similarly dissuading us. For some obscure reason our trench was left unmolested. Gradually the din and the smoke died off; the crater had evidently been licked into the usual shape; and, as though nothing out-of-the-way had happened, every one that could curled up again and dixies of tea went round.

My trench education was proceeding apace, and I acquired a cudgel and a bravado air to accompany me on my watches. The company trench I knew down to the date-card on every vermoral sprayer, but as to the defence scheme my mind was blank. To avoid the wrath of my elders and betters I carried according to precept two signal forms, one marked 'SOS', the other 'GAS'. In effect these would have proved but scraps of paper. At length, one black night, my somnolent trench patrol was disturbed by a fugue of highly unpleasant explosions in no-man's-land. My solution was, immediately, some bombing escapade by

B company – why worry? This sang-froid vanished a
moment later when a corporal came blundering round a
traverse huskily ordering Stand To! 'What's this for?' I
asked, as the corporal, having sent the order along, hurried
back and jumped on the firestep. 'Fritz is bombing B
Company.' My first instinct was to shift to a more comfortable distance! Instead, however, I clambered on the parapet
in a death or glory mood, after the fashion of all the best
recruiting posters, Mills bomb tightly clutched. There was
no occasion to throw even one grenade, as the German
raiding party found B Company warned in time and kept
a respectful distance. Next evening at stand-to, a British
plane arrived – whose, if not the Mad Major's? – and, with
what struck people at that time as the limit in folly and dare-
devilry, carefully planted half-a-dozen bombs in the Boche
trench. So sure were the inmates of the front line in those
days to reap retaliation that we resented such a display, and
indeed hated to hear our own eighteen-pounders hissing
over to the destruction of some suspicious ruin or unsuspi-
cious working party. Whoever piped we paid. All told, this
southern side of the Canal revealed a war of nasty possibilities; there was a tense 'something in the air'; and the
obvious feverish haste of our tunnellers, despite their reluc-
tance to admit anything, did not make us feel on especially
safe ground.

   Between reliefs at Cuinchy the battalion spent two or
three days in reserve at the little village of Annequin. I was
sent down in advance one broiling afternoon, *via* Tour-
bières (vulgo Tubular) Trench and one of the Old La
Bassée Roads. My duty was to get billets, no great dilemma,
the village being well provided with lofts and very little
battered. It was here that a dud shell went through a roof
one evening and the inhabitants repaired the tiles before
going to bed. L— and myself shared a kindly billet – a
cubby-hole only entered by a kind of casement cool with
vine leaves. Thanks to the garden and timely parcels we
lived largely on lobster salad. Our householder was a
miner, one of a batch of forty who daily explored the

galleries under the German lines and kept them in working order. He was a man of few words, but amiable.

There was a huge slag-heap at the south end of Annequin, with a structure not unlike a giant gun on its apex. I believe our observers or flash-spotters used it. At night it was visited by shells of great size, which woke L— up under the idea that our garden was being bombarded. He was unfortunate next day in having to plod up to Cuinchy with a tunneller's fatigue-party, whose work was to stand doubled-up in dark passages of stinking airlessness and water, passing bagfuls of spoil back to the mine-shafts. My luck was in. I walked out that evening to the reedy marshes beyond the houses, and almost became a pagan. The vast serene summer sky, the deepening blue spaces and the silence only surer for the sad rustle of reeds in a little wind; but a deathliness, a poignancy, a sapping stagnancy lying on the mind, embittering the lonely beauty – these influences wove me in a spell. It was as though all nature knew of the war, and saw its future. I became aware of that old certainty-uncertainty: I have surely lived these identical minutes, here, many a time before. The proofs, as ever, passed into oblivion when it seemed that I had at last captured them.

We enjoyed our brief rest at Annequin, but left it for good when we marched up to Cuinchy anew. Daylight relieving still prevailed, despite the hovering sausage-balloons before La Bassée. Small wonder that the forward stretch of communication trench was flattened out and (by way of painting the lily) advertised with a red notice board, DANGEROUS. I remember asking the guide as to the procedure here, and his assurance that even the best people ran by. Our sojourn in the front line I have already described, but of this my sole holiday at Cuinchy there are a few more memories: the midnight deluge of minenwer-fers on our headquarters beneath the brickstack, every one there but my ignorant self expecting to be buried alive next minute; the leaking gas cylinders installed for Loos and now embedded for all time under our parapet; the trench corner covered with rainbow postcards of Edinburgh, Doing His Bit, The Rosary and similar favourite topics; and the miasma of lime, picric, slime and death from every less-used trench. It was a night heavy with greasy fog when we were relieved, and without remorse hobbled down to Harley Street for the last time (as it proved). The men trailed along the tow-path towards Béthune, on the verge of sleep, slouching, speechless. The company commander, whose horse had met him at the gun positions, galloped up and down in anger at the want of 'march discipline', but his propaganda effected little, and neither step nor fours could be kept. Where we halted, we slept in the mud. The first glimmer of daylight stole haggardly over us as we passed the great timber-yards of Béthune, and showed me at what cost to mind and feature we had come through this experience of trench war. My education was advancing, and I now began to wonder what spectacles men might present as they emerged from such fabulous battles as Hooge or Loos. We found the journey back to our tanta-lising rest-billet, Hinges, a very long nine miles, and quietly crawled in and slept.

The men had hardly had time to clean their clayed and water-logged equipment when orders arrived for our early return to the line. No particular regret could be discerned. The war as we saw it fell into two zones: – first, In the Trenches, but less baited and badgered by gorgeous numsculls: second, Out of the Trenches, and suffering from the official terror that we might fall into indolent habits. Thus we were between devil and deep sea. Hingettes (for that was the name of our town end) was a pleasant place, though the smallholders' mania for work had completely domesticated the landscape; there were cherry orchards, and overshadowed white walls, the canal where we swam (in the cause of Organised Games) under the tall-timbered elms, estaminets and small beer abounding, and friendly if apathetic civilians. But there was also a training programme. There was therefore not a wet eye in the company when we once more swept and garnished the already speckless barns (the rules for handing over in a clean and sanitary condition were dumb as to the scarcely clean and sanitary middens so dear to the French farmers), and paraded in full kit for the move. The name 'Neuve Chapelle' at first dismayed me, but L— assured me that our new sector just south of that notorious place was placid in the extreme. Nor was C Company to go straight into the line.

Wherever we might be going, the inhabitants seemed utterly uninterested. Goings-out for them were immediately followed by comings-in; *c'était la guerre*; regiments were all one to folks surrounded with soldiery all day and every day. There was one, however, who betrayed feelings of sorrow at our departure. This was an undergrown, odoriferous mongrel who existed on a chain in the corner of the courtyard. Marie, the linguist, asked when he was last let run, had ventured a hazy recollection that it was about August, 1914. This naïve confession depressed our warm-hearted men. Silent friends had released the decrepit little dog and taken him for runs beyond his wildest dreams, the last two nights. But now these things were at an end. He saw, with remorse at the fickleness of man, the friends departing bag and baggage. Feebly oscillating his tail in an effort to persuade himself that this was only play, but fearing more and more the dreadful truth, he stood with lack-lustre eye among his festering hunks of bully, the very image of misery.

# WAR AND PEACE

How mysterious that after so many years, not inactive, not undramatic, nor passed without much delight and discovery in man and nature, I find myself frequently living over again moments of experience on the Western Front. The war itself with its desperate drudgery is not the predominant part of these memories – I need a more intense word than memories; it is Nature as then disclosed by fits and starts, as then most luckily encountered 'in spite of sorrow', that so occupies me still. The mind suddenly yields to simple visions. Pale light striking through clouds in shafts, like the sunrays of Rembrandt, beyond the mute and destined tower of Mesnil, continues inextinguishably to lure me. The ramping weeds in their homespun fringing the chalky road to grim Beaumont Hamel seem to be within my reach. The waterfowl in the Ancre pools and reed-beds exchange their clanking monosyllables with an aerial clearness, as though there were no others in the ten years between. I think to pick up the rosy-cheeked apples fallen in the deserted, leaf-dappled, grassy gunpits in the orchards of Hamel. And then some word from my companion calls me to lose no more time with our bomb-boxes on the menacing village road.

Perhaps these moments recur according to the season, for it is now autumn, and our share in the Somme fighting began towards the end of a splendid August. Looking back a little, to May and June, I see that this year I was chiefly haunted by seasonable recollections. Now it would be the moon on the white ghost of a house and the white-flowering bush before it in Festubert, with the noise of our ration wagons dying out along the road: now pale cherries, now buoyant apple-blossom brightened our restless camps a mile or two behind, with the guns at their hoarse work close by. Under a plank bridge carrying a trench tramway a nameless runnel whispered, with tiny fish revelling in their brief brilliant existence. Cars and lorries passed apace on the day's business below that twinkling, towering avenue of trees ranked northward out of Béthune – *species aeternitatis*. A sudden sighing came through the swampy sedge behind unholy Cuinchy, to me standing alone near the last dreary silent cottage, under a sky of freakish monster-clouds and rainy sunset. And if this winter is not contrary to the last, I shall often seem to be in Flanders, while the smoky gloom of dull weather gloats upon the dark unfruiting clay, the sweating house-walls, the sulky stained ditches; or the spectral snow-light of dawn will begin to define the long shutters over the broken windows of some punished white château, snow untidily tenanted by genuine 'old soldiers' in charge of stores. Against a bitter blue the jag of St Jean church-tower on the ridge will shiningly overtop the black spikes of trees while we stumble eastward on the glassy pavé; and then, swift relief! I am on Mont Kokereele in the hurling gusts of rain, while the driven, withering bramble claws here and there in the air over the quarry and finds no rest, and the streaming hazels wrestle, until on a sudden the day brightens and we who dig there cease to dig, with words of delight and wonder. For to the south-east a new transparency seems created; the vast plain 'sweeps with all its lessening towers' mile after mile, all calm, all distinct, villages and woods, towns and highways in the beauty of order; some of the gleaming churches mark our long past marchings, and beyond all, like monuments of our experience, we see the dominant Fosses of the black country towards Lens.

That brief phenomenon of magnified and purged sight, when the sun returned through the rain, may best explain what my words cannot – the transforming clarity of such reperceptions as I have exemplified. At such moments one's mortal franchise seems to be enlarged, and a new sphere of consciousness opened. I go a great distance in no time, and hear bells rung in secret. Why should the war leave such effects? God forgive me if they were the only remembrance of the Western Front still vivid to me; in fact they are the singular prologues to long and strenuous enactions of a drama beside which, even in partial and imperfect view, Mr Hardy's *Dynasts* lacks profundity and appalment. They are the puzzling, unanticipated, and ever swiftly concealed side of the picture, and as such I note them, wondering whether ordinary life without the fierce electricity of an overwhelming tempest of forces and emotions could project such deep-lighted detail.

First published in *Nation & Athenaeum*, 6 November 1926; collected in *The Mind's Eye* (London, 1934), where it is dated 1925.

# AFTERTONES

The summer of 1918 drifted past with its eddies of intrigue and dispute and rumour in the camp and the world beyond. It was a camp among ancestral trees, copses, meadows, cornfields bubbling with poppies, windmills on their little heights of goat-grazed turf; besides, the sky was blue and the air southern; yet I screen my eyes from that summer. The delight of being away from France after almost two years of ruins and ever-spreading terror was not itself wholly good; youth, now certain of a short time to live, through some magic dispensation of the War Office, did strange things in a world which it had never had the time to study. Moved by some instinct of spiritual pride, I no sooner arrived in the camp for my six months' respite than I wrote – I 'had the honour to submit' – my application to be allowed to return to France, where such unpleasant German manœuvres were proceeding. The application received no answer, except amused comment from an old major before dinner. I waited a week, then repeated my appeal with more eloquence. This time the Doctor was ordered to examine me; he said that I was unfit to return overseas. It was kind, and before many weeks in the camp it became true. But I was not finished yet. I had the blank half of the warrant which carried me from France, only cancelled in copying pencil. I considered the necessary innocent forgery, which offered no apparent difficulty. The only trouble would be in getting my valise (with books) to the station, eight miles off. However, I already knew a man with a pony-trap. It was merely a question of choosing the night for shooting the moon.

Then one morning I was ordered to assist at a court of inquiry in a town. This had the side-result of a romance, so immediate and complete as to seem love at first sight; my

midnight stratagem and my warm fancy of surprising my
old battalion in some trench or farm buildings behind
Kemmel were set aside. Now began the real grimness of
that shining summer in England. First of all, it was a bad
camp. Next, there was almost always a stealthy hatred
between those who had never 'been out', or had taken one
joy ride behind the battlefield and an overseas-service
chevron, and the returned BEF man, who was presumed to
be no 'soldier'. Then again, the place was merely a mill for
the purpose of crushing the soul out of eighteen-year-old
boys and sending them wholesale into the world's fiercest
furnaces. And there were personal sources of misery. Over-
worked, insulted and ill, some of us broke out into tirades
against our oppressors, and for a time paid heavily for our
uncontrol. It might be amusing now to recall some of these
moments; but not altogether; enough to note how one of
them became tragic. A sergeant-major – a fighting man –
was 'broken' on some ground or other which seemed unim-
portant. On church parade he talked to me of the case, but
did not mention his plan; the next I heard was that he had
committed suicide, leaving letters to say that he hoped his
action might be for the good of his survivors in the camp.
A mutiny followed. After the restoration of 'law and order',
I one day took a draft of two hundred 'eighteen-year-olds'
to the troop train, and was going round the sections,
wishing I was going farther with them, when the Colonel
appeared. It was embarrassing. There were groans and
booings all along the train.

But I delay. When my orders for France at last arrived, I
was in bed, struggling with asthma. The attempt to obey
the orders landed me in hospital, under considerable
distress, and, when I emerged, I was sent on to another
camp, still ill. Days of pale, damp autumn brought
November 11th, and the hooting of sirens in the harbour
below the parade ground on which we were engaged as
usual. Nobody had expected an armistice, and nobody was
excited by it. All assembled round the orderly room,
wishing that the Colonel would celebrate the event with a

speech; but he avoided the historic opportunity. Two or
three days later I was ordered to France, and this time I had
no difficulty in arriving there except the task of shep-
herding several hundred scarcely happy men of all
regiments into their base-camp.

Such journeys were too monotonous to be remembered.
The usual scramble to the engine for hot water, and the
usual rapid hunt for coke and wood round any cabins
beside the line, took place at the halts. I looked out for
Tincques, which had curiously remained in my memory
from the time when we were passing on our way to the old
Somme battle. We detrained at Douai, and I immediately
felt the once-imagined, singular excitement in moving
freely where the German soldier had been billeted. It was
too late; but what would not one have given in 1916 to be
an invisible man for a day or two and see how brother
Boche was enjoying life? The city was not entirely without
suggestion of its dignified history, but the dirtiness of
retreat had yet to be cleansed. It had been on the edge of
destruction, and was now merely a clearing-house for
troops and traffic. The smell of old blankets, wet boots and
wood-smoke came from the dark holes of the barracks in
the November twilight. Leaving the men there with whom
I was joining a battalion still farther on towards Germany,
I took my doubtful way along the canal, examining shell
holes and the litter of machine-gun posts that once – not
many hours ago – made that canal devilish. I saw an empty
building strewn with papers; taking one, I read a German
advertisement for condensed milk. But the packing-cases
all round were torn open and contained no sample. Douai
was like that. By a conservatory door I found what looked
like a book of essays in good binding. But there was no text.
The whole place was the book of life without the inside.

Marching on from this husk of masonry next day, we
crossed a plain of coal-dust tracks and grey grass, of church
spires and chimneys; this trampled country continued for
miles, but presently the villages and lands wore a better
freshness. Here and there a lonely house on a causeway had

been unlucky in the final fighting. One such exposed its deadness at the approach to Hornaing, where I joined my new battalion. The process is always a little unnerving, and to me, with the sense that I ought to have been in France all 1918, it was more than so. However, there were the landmarks plain enough: battalion headquarters and mess, company headquarters, the canteen, the regimental sergeant-major and one's billet. The white and red houses were all much alike; from some of them emerged girls much older than their years, and old men who lived without apparent nourishment. Some of the women of the place were not very well pleased with the peace; generally, yes, but personally, no. I guessed at the circumstances of these strained apprehensive faces. Leaving company headquarters in the first evenings, I could feel much the same difficulty in the abrupt change from a long war to silence. I scanned the eastern darkness as though, if I looked hard enough, the familiar line of lights would be playing there. The silent darkness was in some way worse than those assistants of vengeance. I wanted them. Youth had been subdued to what it worked in.

The old officers of the battalion, who had seen it through, proved to be restless and irritable. They saw disintegration advancing. The men, seeing no special necessity for kicking their heels in a nondescript French village without my 'line of lights', went about their routine without enthusiasm. Drill, marching, inspections, games, concert parties and educational intentions filled in the time. The best diversion was salvaging in woods and marshes and windy beet-fields, but we found little; and my one pair of boots was not equal to these occasions. I was never in a worse billet: the floor was of mud and the enormous mattress was damp beyond help. Rations and supplies altogether became meagre. They had to be brought by rail across the desolation between Arras and ourselves; and now discipline all over Europe was falling to dust, the old battlefield was haunted by looters, military and civilian. Still, the men clubbed together to get what vegetables the village could sell as a supplement to their meals; and the young women whose estaminet one knew would refer with pity to the far worse condition of even the German officers' table a few weeks earlier. 'Soup – our dog refused it.' There was a hope for the future if one considered this kind of remark, and the tenderness in it; but I was glad I was not one of those girls.

In an atmosphere, then, of discontent and indirection, we waited for 1919. Sometimes there was a lively evening, but it depended on make-believe rather than reality. Christmas duly produces a special celebration. It happened, however, that nothing to the purpose could be bought in our district, and with an officer named Browning (not unlike the poet in appearance) and two quartermaster-sergeants, I was sent off in good time to buy the Christmas dinner at Arras. When nowadays I think of buying my own dinner, I am surprised that 'out of all this great big world they'd chosen me' to strike a bargain with a Frenchwoman for a pig, cases of wine, hogsheads of beer and other provisions. But so it was, and I was happy, for the train to Arras, swinging round Douai's red and grey mass across moist green and glittering water-lights, entered the former field of battle in daylight. 'Water, water everywhere', or rather ooze and slush, was working along old cuttings and trenches and holes of the yellow waste. The railway carried over such a swamp was a miracle. It was only just a railway. One could guess at the dead still lying about beyond the banks, even if the choked dug-outs beside the rails were not full of them. Brown mounds of bricks with claws of machinery projecting, and a few huts with their round iron roofs, were all that rose from the famous plain. Roeux Chemical Works might have been any of these low heaps of waste. As we approached Arras, however, the valley of the Scarpe retained a pleasant ghost or two of the leafy past, and lines of slender tree-shapes marked that last pathetic area of no-man's-land and British stand-to billets during the years of steady trenches.

Finding my way into a draughty house in Arras, used as

a club, I signed the book – and above my signature I saw
'G. H. Harrison'. It was almost two years since I had seen
my true Colonel. I looked again: he had been here the day
before. But perhaps he was staying? It was in vain; he had
gone. I waited about, pretending to read, in case he should
be coming back; but he did not, and a great and sudden
hope went to the ground. Reduced afresh to the drifting
mood of those days, I prowled in Arras and saw the landmarks, the still towering Hôtel de Ville and the square with
its grey house-fronts ('Spanish Square'), its enlarged cellars
still looking like man's real home, its barbed-wire barricades. On the whole the German gunners had treated
Arras kindly; but at its eastern bounds the nakedness of the
land began instantly. At present it was still a 'downstairs'
town. The vast rooms aloft would not be easy to return to.
I found a shop open, chiefly selling soap and sardines, in the
ground floor of a fine house, with a flag over the street; but
overhead was vacancy and wreck.

Next day in a cold drizzle we walked out to a village
called Dainville, and inquiring at an estaminet controlled
by two sisters who had not seen four years of the British
soldier for nothing, found that our Christmas dinner could
be supplied. It would cost more than usual – but we had to
have it. One more night in Arras, with old trench-maps and
the *Life of Keats* for company – then back to Dainville, and
concluding the deal. Foully cold as I was, I rejoiced in all
this; there stood a fine farm with stone outhouses – should
have been our billet; there, among half-lowered walls, a
good corner for C Company cookers; there, a pretty
turning, the very thing for marching in by after a day in the
practice trenches. Everything almost was fair or ugly, good
or bad, according to its associations with the spirit of the
BEF. But not everything: there was the citadel on our way
into Arras – as at Ypres there had been some traces of
hornwork and escarpment – to divert the feelings with the
mysterious antiquity of British expeditions to these simple
places.

The slate-tinted reflection of watery paving and

creeping ditches dies away into cold darkness with a wind from the east, from those places which I never knew and which I now conjecture to be more savage and hopeless than any I did know: Gavrelle, and Wancourt, and Roeux. I am in a mental blind alley. This is Arras, full of the domestic echoes of our army, our armies; I was ever an antiquary, and searched the hummocks of Ypres like an Orientalist in Xanadu; I should be going about Arras and reading every syllable of her ancient and modern drama, the comic reliefs and the tragic impacts alike. But again, I am out of tune. It needs the old faces, voices, songs, jests, Colonel Harrison, the sequence and limitation of trench warfare. Meanwhile, the metal of the gaping roof of Arras Station is the wind's dreary harmonium clanking and twanging; the swell of the wind comes flooding through the cold platforms with a mockery of the past or the future habits of railways. From these feelings the arrival of the 'Christmas dinner' on a peasant's cart arouses me; we set about discovering whether there ever will be a train, other than the wind's creation, passing east through Arras, and, if there will, how to put our grimy cargo aboard from its place in the mud.

Midnight, more false rumours through the station, and at last an enormous train; we run our barrels and shoulder our boxes into the already overcrowded trucks of snoring or restless soldiers, tripping over heaps of equipment, and breathing the vapour of mud, sweat, greased leather, trodden food-scraps and dirty water. It is a troop-train resembling rather that of some Balkan war than the not altogether unkempt horse-trucks of our old times in Flanders. A sapper who resented our forcing our goods into the gangway swears at and about us, with dark mouth and insane eye. We hope to be carried in this large coffin to the station nearest our battalion, but are not. A longer stop than usual brings us out on the track, questioning, receiving no replies, false replies; then at last a Frenchman tells us the train goes no farther. We watch him depart with his lantern; we believe he is right, and we unload our belongings. Later, we discover with no mean cunning that some trucks in an archway will go where we wish; the cold and slimy business of getting the 'Christmas dinner' along and forcing it all into the truck high above the track is repeated. The wind is still in the east. The clay-coloured daylight comes.

We arrive! I direct my companions to hurry up the four or five miles of cobbles to the battalion, and send transport; meanwhile I volunteer to watch the stacked cases and casks, which I have paid for on the battalion's account. Black-handed, black-jowled, black-streaked from head to foot, I wait; and an officer of military police comes for me, swinging a heavy revolver in his hand. 'Your papers.' The revolver is not swinging now. I put my dead fingers into my inner pocket and hand him all I have – letters, officer's blue record-book, and what the hell's the matter with you? He with an anxious eye runs over the miscellany; hands part back; saunters with a careful ease into the station, returns and restores my blue book. 'All right. But I was looking for an Australian. Your stuff, I suppose? Ah, the battalion's Christmas dinner.' He retires into his office out of the wind; and I wait. No transport arrives. I am being prepared for influenza, but at last I decide against the process, and I give a call at the guard-room, where a sentry stands over some of His Majesty's property. A present, and a promise, seem to assure me, according to old traditions of this war, that my cases and casks will be looked after by the sentries until I can see why the transport is not on the way; and I depart in relief, with aching eyes and shapeless feet. Unhappily for me, 'this war' ended in November. The transport, some hours later, receives our Christmas luxuries from the guard, but not all – the *blanc* is heavily lightened. I do not gain in reputation on this adventure; I take some days to recover my normal ill-health; and I am twenty pounds out of pocket.

Christmas, nevertheless, arrived and was celebrated; after this the chief purpose of our loitering in France appeared to be celebrating. The old German mess, with its curved and pointed ceilings, was a scene of many endeavours to rebel against the lethargy of armistice. Order went to the ropes more than once; there was a snowy disgraceful midnight when a venerable feud ended in a raid on the Adjutant's billet. In his pyjamas this once Wolseyan youth was hauled into the road and soused in the icy slush. Why, only the instigator knew; but sympathetic assistants were not lacking after repeated draughts of apothecary's wine. Some afternoons we went off by any lorry that passed to Valenciennes or Denain; these excursions showed us little but successions of mine-craters at cross-roads, wood bridges out-flanking the ruins of old and solid ones, and then greasy defaced streets with the wonderful German system of direction-boards conspicuous on houses and corners, and shop-windows coldly crying famine, and mad prices for soap and butter and bread. Duty discovered some varieties for us. Working through the marshy plantations towards St Armand, if we found little but an occasional belt of machine-gun cartridges or a revolver holster (one carried these trophies in with astonishment at the trouble, remembering the prodigious quantity of oddments wasted in and below the Somme battlefield) – wood-ranging here, I say, we had the relics of country beauty about us, and woolly-headed rushes whitened against the blue sky. An airplane plunged into a swamp; out we went with ropes and shovels, like the Lilliputians after Gulliver, and pushed and hauled and squashed and bawled. At night in my damp stable I read Elia and Verlaine, and sometimes my old host, a miner, would look in: 'Monsieur, je viens pour demander ... une voiture pour aller aux mines ... 'y-a du charbon là-bas ...' 'C'est que ma fille est malade ... sans doute vous autres officiers vous avez des fruits sur la table, des oranges – elle désire surtout des oranges.' His son had managed to retain a lean yellow-rimmed bicycle, and went off on it frequently in the direction of the mines. But not for coal. Presently, after a donation of oranges, Mademoiselle recovered, and when I changed my billet in order to obtain a dry room for myself and my Charles Lamb, she came to see the lady of the house, and called on me with that pale face and grey-eyed mysteriousness – she warned me with strange emphasis against one or two of the girls of the parish. A queer world, this world of concealed meanings and magnetic accidents of human desire; how many are the voices that whisper, and could only be answered with years and years of event!

I do not know how my young indolent friend succeeded in keeping his spidery bicycle intact along the terrible roads by the slag-heaps, with the smoke creeping from them. The cobble-stones had been bulged by iron wheels into endless ups and downs, slippery with bad weather. Ordered one day to make a reconnaissance in and about the little town of Bouchain, we rode the usual ironclad army bicycles jarringly along the stumbling-blocks, and it happened that columns of lorries were passing us, sweeping the width almost of the way. We went ahead. Yet none of us was offered music-hall engagements. Bouchain was still Marlborough's town, or the Prince Eugene's. Its waterways defended it on the ancient principle. It slept. And yet it contained large modern barracks and horse-lines; its mill had been turned into a strong tower, where we climbed among the littered explosives, ever curious in our boredom. Along the river was a yard where the carcases of animals had been collected for the service of the German army; many of these carcases were still falling to pieces and mouldering down the banks into the poisoned stream. Vast and brilliant organisation had dug out hidden acres of ammunition dumps in this area, and supplied underground trolleys on their rails, and systems of electricity; these were dead, but the town of Bouchain only slept, and budded trees around the dilapidated houses awaited the spring.

Then came the chance for us. To Germany! and in a couple of days. I went to secure my rights of action once more. Then came a letter from home, with bad news, and urgently recalling me; and almost at once a call to the orderly-room followed. Some time before, our qualifications for being demobilised had been noted down, and I as a 'student' had the chance of being emancipated early. The

Major gave me the order for my departure. I thought of Germany, but the dark message I had had overwhelmed that speculation. I thanked him, and made up my mind. In any event, the period of dreary futility seemed about to end. No more of those 'lessons' from the French interpreter to fill in the evenings; no more blank stares over flat and watery plains. The question now was, what sort of train converted, or began to convert, the soldier into the civilian? Fancy was abroad, and she painted a luxury of travel – talked of cushioned and warmed compartments and a train-ferry to Richborough (it sounded to some ears like Richebourg). The actual journey was so great an ordeal that I wondered if we should see England. Winter returned with fangs; the cattle-truck was without even a brazier, and the wood-fire which I helped to keep going threatened to suffocate us or ignite the whole truck into a moving pyre. Two of the inmates lay under a blanket, ill. They had the new influenza. They died soon after they were 'detrained' on the long bleak siding at the base. I had seen war's ironies when we were in a manner equal to them, but these supplementary strokes were surely out of all bounds. Looking back over 1918 and this opening quarter of 1919, I became desperately confused over war and peace. Clearly, no man who knew and felt could wish for a second that the war should have lasted a second longer. But, where it was not, and where the traditions and government which it had called into being had ceased to be, we who had been brought up to it were lost men. Strangers surrounded me. No tried values existed now. I looked through the gashed linen window of the hut in the waiting-camp at the way down to the boat, deep in snow; I saw the unmanned cookhouses and 'ablution sheds'; and the sunnier hours of my old companionship at Béthune, and even in the valley of the Ancre, with their attendant loyalties and acceptances, seemed like sweet reason and lost love. Marching down to the docks, at the side of a great column of weary soldiers of all sorts, I was suddenly pulled up by an officer of about my own age, who, in a trembling voice, demanded that I

should at once improve the march discipline of the multitude, none of whom I had ever seen before. The Base
Commandant, he warned me, would be on the look-out as
we passed his headquarters. The Base Commandant had
given orders that the marching of the troops should be
maintained at the highest standard. 'Keep in your fours!',
'Pick up the step there !' – but I did not succeed in reviving
the martial spirit in those pestered, loaded, scrambling
ranks with my thin reminders of a fantastic chivalry.

First published as 'A Postscript' in *The Legion Book*, edited by Captain H.
Cotton Minchin (London, 1929); collected as 'Aftertones' in *The Mind's
Eye* (London, 1934).

# THE SOMME STILL FLOWS

It was a sunny morning, that of July 1st, 1916. The right notes for it would have been the singing of blackbirds and the ringing of the blacksmith's anvil. But, as the world soon knew, the music of that sunny morning was the guns. They had never spoken before with so huge a voice. Their sound crossed the sea. In Southdown villages the school-children sat wondering at that incessant drumming and the rattling of the windows. That night an even greater anxiety than usual forbade wives and mothers to sleep. The Battle of the Somme had begun.

This battle on the southern part of the British line over-shadowed everything else. Even Ypres fell quiet. The three nations most prominently concerned on the Western Front concentrated their force in the once serene farmlands of Picardy. Their armies had arrived at a wonderful pitch of physical and spiritual strength. They were great organiza-tions of athletes, willing to attempt any test that might be ordered. If the men of the Somme were probably unri-valled by any earlier armies, the materials and preparations of the battle were not less extraordinary. Railways, roads, motor transport, mules, water supply, aircraft, guns, mortars, wire, grenades, timber, rations, camps, telegraphic systems – all multiplied as in some absurd vision. Many of you who are reading now still feel the fever of that gath-ering typhoon.

Such monstrous accumulations, and transformations of a countryside which in the sleepier period of its war had been called 'The Garden of Eden', could not be concealed from the intended victims. Surprise on the large scale was impossible. But the British devised local surprises; rapidly dug jumping-off positions; field guns waiting to fire from the front trenches; the terrific mine ready to go up at La

Boisselle. The defenders also had their secrets prepared for
July 1st.

At last the moment came for mutual revelations.
Villages, wiped out in a few hours, earned reputations for
hopeless horror when our men rose in the daylight from
their already destroyed positions and moved to capture
them. Some of them they did capture. Few who survived
long enough under German guns and machine-guns to
enter the trenches opposite could have retained any illu-
sions. They found themselves in a great trap of tunnels and
concrete and steel rails and iron entanglements. From holes
in the land they had crossed, from higher ground north and
south, from untouched gun-pits, these isolated men were
also wiped out. I knew a colonel whose hair turned white
in this experience. I knew Thiepval, in which battalions
disappeared that day. I knew Thiepval Wood, before which
in the mud of November were withering bodies of the
British and German combatants of July 1st.

The outbreak of the Somme battle may be described as
a tremendous question-mark. By the end of the day both
sides had seen, in a sad scrawl of broken earth and
murdered men, the answer to that question. No road. No
thoroughfare. Neither race had won, nor could win, the
War. The War had won, and would go on winning. But,
after all the preparation, the ambition, the ideals and the
rhythms of these contending armies, there could not be any
stopping. Tomorrow is always another day, and hope
springs eternal. The battle of the Somme would continue
from summer to winter. The experiment of the century
must be repeated, varied, newly equipped. Perhaps luck
would play a part. Perhaps external conditions would affect
these machine-gun emplacements, and the lucky lads from
Adelaide or Sunderland walking onward through the
explosions.

Accordingly, what had been begun on July 1st became a
slow slaughtering process; the Somme might have been a
fatal quicksand into which division after division was drawn
down. In order to illustrate that remark, I am going to

sketch the history of the division in which I served during the offensive. Though we were far north of the battlefield in June 1916, we nevertheless came under its fiery influence; for, on the last day of June, we were sent into a 'minor operation' as they called it, with the object of keeping back German troops and artillery from the real affair. Our brigade assaulted; crossed a flat water-meadow, full of deep dykes and thick barbed wire, under every kind of fire; and a great many of us were dead or wounded within a couple of hours. 'Like a butcher's shop,' said a plain-spoken private to the general next day. When we had to some extent recovered from this minor operation, the powerful and ominous words came round, 'We're going South'.

War is not all war, and there lies the heart of the monster. 'Going South' was at first more like a holiday adventure than the descent to the valley of the shadow. I still make myself pictures of that march, and could not guess at any summer days more enchanting. The very fact that, after ceaseless rumours and contradictions, we were now certainly destined for the Somme battle made us shut our minds to the future and embrace the present. We marched with liberal halts through wooded uplands, under arcades of elms, past mill-streams and red and white farms; and, as we marched, we sang. Not even the indifferent map-reading of the boyish officer at the head of the battalion could damp our spirits. What were kilometres? At twilight we took over our billets in clay-walled barns, or farmhouses with vine-leaves at the windows and 'café, monsieur' at any moment. Every man knew his neighbour. Never was such candour or such confidence.

We stayed longer at the hamlet which provided our training-ground. Indeed, its chalky hillsides were said to be precisely similar to our future share of the Somme battle-field. In an interval of our successful attacks on the dummy trenches of our ghostly enemy, we lay down by companies while some particularly well-nourished experts from General Headquarters eulogized the beauty of the bayonet. We went to sleep. Presently rainy weather set in, but when we continued our journey to the battle the sun burned and the dust rose along the road. It was towards the end of August.

After several postponements we made our first appearance in the fighting. We did not know, most of us, that the lines which we had dreams of capturing had been attacked on July 1st. But, as I stared across a valley at the German positions, a day or two before our action, I was puzzled by a small heap of what was clearly British barbed wire, on its original reels, a long way behind the enemy's front trench. In the cold early mist of September 3rd our division went over. A few astonishing officers and men fought their way to those coils of wire. One or two returned from them in the evening, by which time history had repeated itself. The shattered battalions withdrew from the valleys and ridges still echoing with bombardment and the pounding of machine-guns. The Somme had pulled us under once, and we emerged just gasping. Somewhere to the south there had been a success.

We did not withdraw far. We quickly returned to the line and remained in the trenches, from which two mighty attacks had been launched, week upon week. South, there was still a vague hope. Trenches were said to be changing hands beyond Thiepval Hill, which still frowned upon our ragged remains of trenches. We witnessed and heard furious attacks in that direction, rolling smoke, bursts of flame, soaring signal-lights; but these closed in autumn darkness. One day a sensation was caused. Down there in the south the British had made an attack with Tanks, which we understood to be as big as houses and capable of pushing houses down. Then the Somme was still a promising experiment!

For our own next attack we had no assistance of tanks. It was now a long age since July 1st and its blue skies. Yet October 21st was a still, frosty day. A surprise was reserved for our opponents: we were to attack a few minutes after noon. We did. Some of us had now seen three attacks, others had just arrived from the barrack-squares, where sacks of straw are nimbly transfixed by unshelled and unbombed soldiers. We took our trench, and were then submitted to artillery concentration, which went on two days. There were enough of us left to hand over the conquered ground to the 'next for the barber', and to crawl back through endless shell-holes and dead. The captured trench was partly floored with bodies.

Almost at once we were in the line again, and after some days of curious peace we moved to a desperate mud-field east of Thiepval – one of the classic terrors of the Western Front. The year was breaking up now. The craters were swimming with foul water. What was left of the trenches became lanes of yellow and blood-brown slime, deeper than our average height. The tracks beside them were usually smoking with accurate gunfire. The alternative was, generally, to be blown to pieces or to be drowned. After several days of the Schwaben Redoubt, with the corpses choking the dugout entrances, we were informed of another surprise arranged for the enemy. Our division was to take part in a large attack. This occurred on November 13th. The division surpassed itself, capturing ground and one labyrinth of dugouts with many hundreds of Germans in them. Still, there was no sign yet of the fabled green country beyond the Somme battle. That evening I was sent forward with a runner on a reconnaissance. It was growing dark, a drizzling rain was steadily increasing, and on every side was the glare and wailing and crashing of bombardment. We passed through the new posts of the British advance, shivering in water-holes, and then we went blindly astray. After our painful wandering through the barrages of two artilleries and the crazy ruins of trench and battery systems, we were lucky enough to find a way back. That night, retracing our adventure with the colonel and his maps, we found that we had been in the outskirts of a village named Grandcourt. Grandcourt! We felt a little proud. But it came out that some British soldiers had made their miraculous way to that village through the German forts and fire on that remote summer's morning, July 1st.

After this winter battle we left the Somme – but who were 'we'? Not those who had marched south in the time of ripening orchards; a very different body of men. We had been passed through the furnace and the quicksand. What had happened to this division was typical of the experience of all divisions, in all the armies. There is no escape from the answer given on July 1st to the question of the human race. War had been 'found out', overwhelmingly found out. War is an ancient impostor, but none of his masks and smiles and gallant trumpets can any longer delude us; he leads the way through the cornfields to the cemetery of all that is best. The best is, indeed, his special prey. What men did in the battle of the Somme, day after day, and month after month, will never be excelled in honour, unselfishness, and love; except by those who come after and resolve that their experience shall never again fall to the lot of human beings.

First published in *The Listener*, 10 July 1929 (broadcast on 1 July); collected in *The Mind's Eye* (London, 1934).

# WE WENT TO YPRES

I looked south-east out of the bedroom window, which was lofty, but approachable by means of a kind of fire-step. Those were the hills that knew so much. That would be Verbrandenmolen, with a new windmill. From the railway cutting past Hill Sixty, puffs of steam rose in white clouds and thinned away. It was a suspicious appearance, in that particular spot – but it really meant nothing unkind. Southward, Mount Kemmel was green almost as in the days before the bonfire of 1918, and I thought I could make out the toy observatory among the trees. Summer's evening light was over all the place; not casting its splendours, but, as I would have had it, veiled in soft rainy warmth.

Nearer, below, was the railway station of Ypres, a humble structure which no one would have mistaken for a town hall. I had never stepped from a train there until this evening. Indeed I had only seen two or three ration-trains in this city; they used to occur, without lights, beside an old timber-dump on the west side. They amazed us, first by arriving, and then by getting away. But here was the correct, authorized, official station doing its duty. Nothing strange, of course, to see young clerks, schoolgirls, soldiers on furlough, market-dames emerging past a ticket-collector into a cobbled Place. But I found it a little strange.

Just round the corner I looked for company headquarters. The last time I turned that corner, a shell had killed two men beneath the shining shell-cases hung as gas-gongs. I could not now discover which was the house above the still distinctly-remembered basement, any more than which was the house with the painted swans on its shrapnel-spattered inner walls, or that which supplied me with a few books as I balanced along the unfallen beams of the upper storey.

But things like that must be. At least I was geographically 'about right'. The Ramparts were not so baffling. Lovers sat on the benches above them, and below, and a pike made a dash among the lilies; but I knew the curves and inlets of the moat, and remembered the setting of the churches, St Pierre and St Jacques, between the Lille and the Menin Gate. Of our former shelters, most traces were gone. The stylish canvas latrine, for instance, which was specially reserved for the 'G.O.C., —th Inf. Bde', no longer stood like a lodge at the entrance to our estate – the brick vault traversing the Ramparts. But that vault was there, with a doorway (padlocked). Looking in, I saw that the far end (on which German telescopes once were pointed) had been opened, to afford a passage to an allotment on the edge of the moat.

But older soldiers might have found still more of their Ramparts. My walks along the top had almost all been in the flame-tormented dark, and now, without embarrassing the ardent couples in their tenancy, I could see by the quiet light an unsuspected staircase of Vauban's, leading down to a dugout that will probably be there if ever it is wanted again. The Lille Gate no longer gave me prospect of a smoke and drink downstairs with the 'Electric Light Company', but its internal architecture, perhaps even older than Vauban, seemed to be in existence. Where were our swans that haunted these recesses? The new Menin Gate hardly seemed to have the perpetuity of the Ramparts each side. Its marble was not 'to the manner born'. Raising my eyes to the names of those who knew it well, the first I could read was that of my friend C., and I grudged that and the other names. The Ramparts did not seem to want them. How intensely we want them!

Another day; it is the weather in which Waterloo was fought, and the scene is similar, I imagine, with all its peasant property, its velvet-green, its tethered red-sided heifers, its muddy pavements outside drab beer-houses at crossroads. Everything, except the tag ends of villages and the track, seems richer by the harrowing of war. It is ridiculous to be

depressed by the triumph of life, but I feel a little grey as I
move in this vernal world, marvellously re-flourishing. I am
grateful to the low drumfire of the thunder, and the
sudden, cold, slashing, thorough rainstorm which makes us
crouch under an outhouse wall in Zillebeke, a stone's throw
from the church. But this moment of contact is ended by
an enterprising taxi-driver, who has had word of visitors
*walking* in Zillebeke. He pulls up to propose the advantages
of his vehicle, and the good sense of employing him to
show us Mount Sorrel, Hill Sixty, and a series of other
names. Feebly we assent. After all, the war is over, infinitely
over, and we are half-drowned and (who would have
forseen it?) weary of a couple of miles of stone road. We
know by now what he means by Hill Sixty. It will be a
souvenir shop, a window displaying several brands of beer,
a slippery patch of ground enclosed by wire fences, and a
placarded hole or two like the rubbish-dumps of any
village, but without so much iron.

This view proved to be correct enough. But before
leaving Ypres, we had resourcefully noticed an advertisement of Original Fire Trenches in this neighbourhood. I
mentioned that to our driver. He was prepared for it. He
was going there. The taxi drew up near a hovel or two,
with directions to the trenches; but before one could set
eyes on those memorials, a small fee was payable. It was
received by a 'character', a tall, wild, voluble young man
like a backwoodsman, with a remarkable command of
English. He at once began speaking enthusiastically of the
discovering of remains of all sorts, especially bodies. He
complained (in such a way as said 'However, we live') that
it was far from Ypres, and so the ten francs allowed by the
authorities for the bringing home of a British soldier was
not easy money. 'The German Government,' he said,
'don't pay us anything, so we don't trouble to report the
German bodies we find.' He expected approval, but one
of us was a German, and I said, 'But these German
soldiers were fine men, and ...' 'Oh yes, sir,' he rapidly
interrupted, catching the idea, 'yes, very fine soldiers. Now

these are the trenches, and I am today opening another communication trench.' A small boy with a shovel, at these words, began scooping out a little mud and water from the winding ditch. 'You see this boot? Those are the original toes in it. There, look, that's the original galvanized iron.' 'What's this trench called?' 'Warrington C.T.,' he guessed. I had been in these trenches before, and had been paid for it! 'That's a bit of an ammunition box ...' The small boy again like an automaton flung out his shovelful, but drew a blank.

The least transformed war-ground at Ypres, last summer, was that along the canals, both that from the Lys, and the Yser Canal. Not that the lineaments of war were obvious. But there was not yet a racial reconquest. The birds and frogs in the reeds were unmolested, the waterway was doing nothing but lie in the sun and rain; nothing of our old shelters stood along the banks, but you could find a wrenched and pierced length of roofing in the soft soil where, here and there, it showed the ancient arrival of a shell. We found a shell even. Along those banks, probably half a million shells came down. Trespassing away, we found some wooden posts along the little Yperlee, once part of dugouts in which generals discussed Z Day; and here was a concreted doorway, leading nowhere. I pushed it, and a slab of concrete promptly tumbled into the Yperlee. Farther along, there was more concrete – the medical dugouts at Essex Farm. These by all the laws should have ceased to exist twelve years earlier. They stood then in a very 'windy corner', and as I passed them, though not pausing to reflect, I thought that they would soon be struck by something larger than usual. No – here they were in a warm day of blue skies and flowery breezes, themselves dark and dank. But you could lean against them, and they did not fall. I hope they have not fallen. At least, if they have done, they had an uncommon lease of life in the days when Flanders was ejecting Britain and Germany before her army of small-holders, and preparing the Grand Place of Ypres for new wars of liberty. The walls blazoned forth the doings of a swollen Red Giant, who was booting a top-hatted bourgeois in black, clean out of the immortal Salient.

First published in *Time and Tide*, 7 February 1930; collected in *The Mind's Eye* (London, 1934).

# THE EXTRA TURN

G., in a moment of weary activity, has repaired the primitive neglected gramophone which, I remember, he resolutely carried home and demobilized from the Western Front. It is precisely similar to one which was a friend of ours in 1916, on the edges of that battle of the Somme which was so unfavourable to gramophones and their owners. As soon as he produced the specimen from his perpetual salvage dump, I knew that there would be trouble; and when he had succeeded in making it rehearse a few pieces – Beethoven's 'Minuet', the 'Largo', Pierné's 'Serenade' seemed inevitably to come forward – the trouble was in full flood. But G., who has no real passion for antiquity, then compelled his machine to be comparatively modern, and we heard the loud, hot, joyful lyric of the 'King's Horses, and Men' –

They're not out to fight the foe,
You might think so, but O dear no!
They're here because they've got to go
To put a little pep into the Lord Mayor's Show.

I left them at it; I had been called to a distance where the King's Men, it seemed, were still engaged in shows of another sort.

You see the trouble. One does one's best to live with the date, but accidents happen. Happy are those who on January 1st, 1932, are able to belong to January 1st, 1932. Perhaps I must surrender. I hate this large calendar here. The spirit in which it and a dozen others were given to me was exquisite. I could picture L. at the stationer's, trying to select the One that – subject to little preferences of L., I mean – would suit my taste, eyesight, study-table, and forgetfulness. But what is the use to me of this vast red warning? No wonder if I have not torn off the leaves for a fortnight. The numbers on them vary – I admit it; but they are all one.

For, if it had not been the gramophone, the baffling of my sense of time present would have arrived in another form. It was lucky for me that, when I shared the 'Standing Room Only' the other evening, Mr George Robey had changed his stage character so boldly from that of years ago, and was principally a 'German musical phenomenon' (and some of them guffawed when this expert confessed 'he could not spick English so well what he could before der War!'). Had Mr Robey been resuscitating the songs from *The Bing Boys* .... But, I think, my luck was fair that evening. How immensely hard our gramophone worked in 1916, obedient to the commands of *The Bing Boys*! How maliciously and gaily did our colonel, who had some doubts as to the efficiency, in the matter in hand, of Liberal leaders, recite and variegate that stanza:

> In Parliament to-day when they get into a stew,
> When they're all mixed up, and they don't know what
> > to do,
> Mr. Asquith says, in a voice *serene* and *calm*,
> 'Another little drink wouldn't do us any harm'.

The same colonel – time and the Bavarians over the way permitting – would listen to the 'Largo', and assert presently that for him there was one of the outstanding and permanent things in the shaken world.

But I have not yet told you where and when our gramophone was at its best. You may not know the Somme battlefield (beetfield now, I trust, and orchards even). Somewhere out to the east of Amiens there was a village called Beaumont Hamel, on a broad chalk hill that descended to a once romantic millstream, the Ancre. Beaumont Hamel being in its last days a fortress, and indeed Germany's masterpiece of brainwork, spadework and ironwork, we were restricted to trenches a little apart from its western tree-stumps. And beautiful trenches too, but for an ugly corner or two; and over them the September sun burned, and a young line of aspens silvered with musical restlessness at their western entry. And over them the guns made argument, and into them the fires descended. The season-change of apple boughs and berried hedgerows tapestried the sky behind us, where we lived in a kind of log-cabin and white house in one, annexed to the trench called Second Avenue. Northward we saw the grey structures of another local headquarters position, White City, and the lower bricks and windows of a sugar refinery. Southward, we cared not to look too often. It was not the slanted crucifix above the tombs of *cultivateurs* there, or the displaced marbles and wreaths, that caused this peculiarity in us. It was the battle of the Somme, in which we had lately been plunged very powerfully – a mile south, two miles; a couple of hours down the road and round and up again where roads ended.

Meanwhile, Beaumont Hamel was reasonably tolerant of us. There might be an outburst now and then, but much might be said on both sides. On our territory, just above the old Beaumont Road (which in those days might have proposed to the tourist with just as much credit an access to Saturn), a cave existed under a hillock, with a crevice in the roof, through which a heavy trench-mortar shot up its Flying Pigs. These tinned projectiles, even when they collide with nobody in particular, have all the elements of unpopularity about them. The unpopularity extends even to those who handle them. F., how often have I regarded you, with all your blameless life and religious inheritance, as not a fit companion for youth! It was Sidneian virtue in our colonel to invite even F. into the log cabin for a drink and, a tune.

Often – we stayed weeks in those trenches – the evening came on nearly as still as in Milton's vision, and guests arrived for dinner and the gramophone; while the green starlight gleamed, and greener pearl-chains of tracer shells went up from somewhere at something in the air. Pratt the gunner, with his indiscretions from Brock's Benefit and its explosive neighbourhood, was the favourite visitor. I do not know quite why I am telling my reader these things;

Pratt is dead and gone, and after all, we hardly knew him ourselves in point of – the Calendar. We only held those trenches a month. But, I conjecture, there is a reason; on shipboard, they say, people soon fall in love; in war, you fall in friendship, and know your neighbour as you probably will never do otherwise. So, there was Pratt, all courtesy and fun, and Harrison, delighted, though hidden secrets of responsibility and anticipation gnawed at him, and Lintott, manliest, wisest of adjutants, and Millward just returning from an 'internal economy' walk round the companies, and myself half lost in the happiness of being thought useful and even then justifying it by plying the handle of the gramophone. 'How's Colonel Allardyce?' 'Well, sir, a five-nine nearly spoiled his bath yesterday – he sends you his regards, he's sorry he blew your front line up the other night, but as you know there is no instance in this Division of a gun firing short … "'Crazier Bray" once more! "I'll have the matter attended to, even in the cannon's mouth."' 'Yes, that's what young James said (he's nineteen), "The trouble with George, sir, is that he suffers from extreme youth". – Augur!' 'Sir!' Enter Augur with his jacket off, grey shirt-sleeves rolled up – pleasant attitude of standing at attention vaguely shadowed. 'Is Mr Pratt's signaller having his supper?' 'He is sir.' 'Good. Now, Rabbit, recite your favourite poem from Alfred Lester. Or Horace. Or one of your own. He's a shy fellow, this Rabbit.'

If the gramophone handle were abused and ceased to have its natural effect, the interruption in the music did not last long. A good battalion could do anything short of smoking German ration tobacco. Sergeant Seall, though his main concern was with runners and messages, knew all about disobedient gramophones, and soon restored the instrument to begin revolving afresh this overture, that gavotte, that comedian's jest about fire-engines and railway porters. There was no mutability in it; it defied casualty. I shall expect to read one Sunday in the *Observer* a passage like this: 'Amiens. A peculiar ghost-story is reported from Auchonvillers. M. Henri Delabière, clearing some beanhaulm near the old Crucifix, was surprised to hear, as though from a land drain, the strains of a gramophone. Under the impression that a joke was being played on him, he returned to the village; but the next evening passing the same spot, he again heard the mysterious notes. M. Delabière proceeded to Mailly-Maillet and communicated these occurrences to a lady in that town, who took occasion to visit the scene at the same hour, and, having some knowledge of English, was able to pronounce that the principal tune was named "If You Were the Only Girl in the World". Indeed, Mlle R— recalled that this very song had been sung to her on more than one occasion in the year 1916, while she was in charge of an estaminet at Doullens, patronized by the British soldiers. Whence, however, the music now heard near Auchonvillers was caused, she could not explain. A full report of the matter is being drawn up by the Phantomological Society of Amiens.'

No; it is all still. The gramophone that went with us from Béthune to the Somme battle and thence to the Convent at Ypres – one of many thousand itinerant musicians of those days – is obsolete. I must discipline myself in this question of winding up clocks and tearing off the sheets of my calendar. There he goes again, 'One Hour of Love with You'; and we are about to return from Mont Noir to the Menin Road in the collapse of 1917, and the floodgates of heaven (is that sour sky heaven?) are open, and the battle is to continue. 'I'd give the sunshine to gaze in your eyes.' Why did they like that amorous ditty at that sunless moment? I found it unsatisfactory, and I still do. I must protect myself. After all, this is not my gramophone, nor, whatever its history prior to 1919, is it our own authentic, distinct, separate, original instrument. On the whole I think that at an auspicious minute I will give the handle one turn too many. Probably G. will not again feel an impulse to repair the relic. I will contrive not to ask him to do so.

First published in *The New Keepsake* (London, 1931); collected in *The Mind's Eye* (London, 1934).

# FALL IN, GHOSTS

*An Essay on a Battalion Reunion*

*Alonzo.* Captain!
*Martino.*            I am glad to kiss
Your valiant hand, and yours; but pray you, take notice,
My title's changed, I am a colonel.
*Pisano.* A Colonel! where's your regiment?
*Martino.*       Not raised yet;
All the old ones are cashier'd, and we are now
To have a new militia: all is peace here,
Yet I hold my title still, as many do,
That never saw an enemy.

Massinger's Bashful Lover

The battalion had halted in the light shade of the line of poplars, which began to look a little unkempt aloft. Rifles had been piled into the usual little pyramids, men had seated themselves on their heavy packs, except the cooks and others with immediate duties. The cooks had lost no time. Their fires already breathed blue spires of smoke into the calm but subtle sky. Beneath that sky, two empires were at war. One village further to the east, and you would have seen the furrowings and burnings of that dismay on the face of the land. Here there was not such obvious evidence. The big grey house with deep white window-sills at the turn of the field path, the farm with its square-set sheds and stalls among other poplars, the crucifix surmounting the steps of granite in the middle of the root-fields, the clean causeway, the trickling land-drain under the culvert did not report the imminence of an enemy. On a closer inspection, it would have occurred to you that some Rembrandtesque cabins among close canopies of apple-

boughs, low brown cabins unbrightened with the spirit of
the green season, must be the homes of guns. Those new
ditches, with their hurdled sides, leading to circular work-
ings and mounds of whitening earth and mazy wire fences,
were nothing agricultural. The group of cottages at the
crossroad a few hundred yards off had not, certainly, been
attacked by a common fire; their beams and laths were
indeed a little blackened, but something had juggled them
into a wild series of angles against the daylight.

'What the deuce are you sitting here for, young man, and
watching your cooks make all this smoke? Get round and
stop them.' The youth looked up at his friendly tyrant,
jumped to his feet and said, 'I'm sorry, sir, I was told that
the men must have tea, and – ' 'Yes, that's right, but for
heaven's sake tell those fellows to keep their smoke under.
We're only two miles here from the German line.' The
youth scurried away to the problem of preventing that
smoke-column from the cookers; which solved itself. Tea
was up; dixies were on the way round the leaning and
laughing and contemplating and dozing company. There
was no need for more smoke. He returned to the little
group of officers, and accepted his mug of tea without
apprehension. The Major had puzzled him afresh by his
blend of correctiveness and sympathy. The officers here –
Green with his pipe and map, Stephenson with his back
against Green's – were commenting on the place chosen for
the halt, and the prospect of an aeroplane's catching sight
of the whole move.

'Packs on!' The interval was over; the quiet morning had
failed to conjure up any burst of horror. The motorcyclist
from Brigade had come and gone in bumping progress,
delivering the orders; and now the battalion was moving
with the most stylish ease it could along the cambered,
cobblestone Rue d'Aubépine. The hamlet with its shells of
houses and its beds and mattresses dangling over its
crooked walls – does so little plaster, and so little timber, and
a front door and a bureau make a dwelling? – was left
behind. 'You may smoke.' With rifles slung over their shoul-

ders, the men were in good mood. Songs sprang up, grew loud and rival songs intervened; you hardly knew which choir to join. 'Who were you with last night?' 'England was England ...'? Heads moved left and right as interest arose with the approach to common life. Civilians were met; one respectable Frenchman had such a fierce goatee moustache that the battalion with one accord, in the purest spirit of *entente cordiale*, set up a magnificent 'Maa-aa'. 'See that, Nobby? That's an Estaminet. Where the MMPs stop.' 'O, a Rest-a-minute. Well, I'm willing.' 'This country was made for war, sir. All these places were built to be knocked over easy. When did you see a shanty like that in England?'

'Appree la Guer fee*nee*.'

'There was a fellow in the lot that relieved us, sir, who'd been in the secret service.' 'Why, that's odd; they say there's a fellow in this division whom the Germans are after and who's only safe up the line.' 'Well, perhaps that's the same man: he said von Krupp's hands were all going on strike this year.' 'Arthur, you're an optimist.' 'What did you call me?' 'The first seven years will be the worst.' 'These Alley-mans never wanted war, you bet.' 'Why don't the Pope stop it?' 'Ah, he's a Roman Catholic. Jerry's Protestant.' 'Ah.' 'Old Captain Rattle's beginning to sweat, look! – No, but why can't Freemasonry stop it?' 'ESSARS two kilos; bet you we're in the line again tonight.' 'What? Not going *this* road. They say we're off to guard iron rations at le Havre.' 'Well, every time there's anything on the poor old Ninth click. Hi, there's old Sergeant Nell. Hey, hey, Sergeant, how's the rum, how's the wife and family? – What, don't you remember him? He's been on some claims stunt since we was at Barnham Barracks. Nice job, with that bike. Bet they don't turn *him* out at eight.' 'March to attention!' At the entrance to another village, on the bank, there is the galaxy of command and authority which they know as a considerable element in their war. The General has a glit-tering eye above that collation of ribbons.

In such circumstances, many made their true discovery of the battalion, the large family, to which they had come as not very confident strangers. Good fortune and a few months improved the matter, you recollect, beyond all dreams. There had never been mutual understanding like it in your experience. Wherever you went, you saw a friend; if you drifted into the quartermaster's stores out of the line, there was this lively pleasure of welcome and acceptance; if you called to the snipers in their lair in the saphead, there would be a cheerful response, the sackcloth that hung behind them and their soon closed loophole would soon be drawn aside to admit you, and you sat with them and their telescope in the knowledge that they were glad. Every face and every name was intensely known to you, while that life lasted. You grew to judge men either as desirable or undesirable additions to the family; the young pioneer officer, for example, with the sly, quiet epigrams and the unhurrying, entire control of a strung-out party of spadesmen, never seemed to belong to his own unit; he was yours by rights. The brilliantly invincible transport officer of the next battalion, who seemed to turn up anywhere – a shell exploded, and there *he* stood, with his latest irony to tell you – was a part of your transport officer's existence, and one implied the other. Some faces seemed destined to go on for ever, for a battalion could not be suffered by whatever powers then ruled the mad hour to be quite extinguished or supplanted. In them was concentrated, after the frightful desolations of battle upon battle, the beauty, faith, hope which flowered in the word: the battalion. Or was this an illusion? Very few men lived through the full career of any unit (that perhaps is the more scientific term); and, as those familiar faces became more remote, others became the typical, life-giving, and sustaining presences with – was it the same battalion? It had the same number and place in the line. It was thought the same; but, perhaps, each of us knew a battalion not quite identical with any other man's, though we served long enough together and borrowed one another's army correspondence-books for months and months. Here before me is such a book, a legacy from one with whom I have lain in chilly weeds ahead of our line, have walked and talked in the cathedral of St Omer, have waited in our den of a company headquarters for the downward crash of daybreak's secret. If any two ever shared a battalion as an unmistakable spiritual and corporal estate, he and I were the two. But what does his book tell me?

It says, I fancy, that there came a time when, long before I was struck off the strength, as they called it, before I ceased to help the permanent Fred Worley to screw in the long wire-pickets on dark nights, *my* battalion was a conception of the past. How fast the war had used up the burnt-offerings! Possibly the battle of the Somme, which had almost entirely transformed the roll of officers serving with us, had at once matured and written the epitaph for my conception; if not that, then the opening of the savage squalid battle for Passchendaele had marked the conclusion of that honourable love. Is it so even in normal life, in that kaleidoscope, which goes by the name of Peace? I begin to conjecture it. Your world, or mine – would you claim continuity for the references of the term? Turning over my friend's book of the autumn of 1917 I do not find the name of one who had been, to him and to me, the first and last reverence as often as we repeated the word, the battalion. He was gone. His successor, beloved by him, schooled by him, alert in his ideals, was with us, as he had been throughout; for the transition to a certain homelessness of mood, the fault was not his. War like a cataract had swept the battalion away, was doing the same for the battalion that had still formed itself up; I do not know most of these names, though I must have seen the men. This carbon copy of a letter addressed (I believe) to me is as though I were reading lists of the wounded at Fontenoy or Malplaquet:

3 a.m. Gas shell bombardment still in progress though shelling slight. Casualties as under to above hour.

15767    Cpl. Johnson, V. H.    Wounded.

15193    Pte. Sendall, C.            "
8420      "   Gilbert, S.              "
15171     "   Partridge, W.  Gassed, died.
5837      "   Huggett, G.  Gassed.
          (Gas masks blown off in these cases.)
1539     Pte. Henry, C.  Wounded.
15199     "   Wilkinson        "

Then there is the recommendation of 2271 Pte Simmons, A.A., for the following action in an attack which I too was obliged to take part in – and I had for the past fifteen years never thought of this extraordinary youth as being in *my* battalion.

> Single-handed killed 4 enemy officers, sending in valuable information promptly early in the attack. Later took charge of night listening posts, two nights running, and was killed by a sniper by the Steenbeck.

What was he like, when did he join us, was he with V— that morning when V— and I laughed hysterically in the trenches just left by the Germans to us and the German barrage? Not a sound.

Did the same obliterative effect happen to you, do you think it would have done? If 'household gods plant a terrible fixed foot', so do some associations; they have a hatred for anything like superannuation and substitutes. In that dizzy period of dreams, rumours, upheavals, fears, escapades, vanities, immeasurable moments, apprehensions, that which one had gained as a sheltering, steady, warm abiding-place in nature became especially precious. At one time it was actual, present, daily and hourly – and when that date was expired, among the other dreams this dream stood long, the shadow of a great rock in that weary land. The odd thing is, I suppose, that a number of us, who are no very enthusiastic metaphysicians, still cling to our rock; and, without noticing what we are doing, we submerge our individual differences of experience and

choice, and the horribly rapid mutations of the war history
of an infantry force as a human group. We come together,
once a year, without allusion to the details of our own
former shares of the history that concerns us, and we reanimate – the battalion. It is our quaint attempt at catching a
falling star.

In my opinion we do it very tolerably. We have – at
present – more qualifications than might have been
expected. At one of our evenings, this fact was expressed
with abrupt emotion by one of us who had been 'in foreign
parts' and had only just heard in time that there was a
regular reunion of our camp. 'Gentlemen,' he began, 'I am
glad to be here; it is surprising to see that so many of us are
alive. No ghosts here? nobody feeling a little out of his
element?' And, I thought, some of the diners glanced
round the room as if they half felt one or two figures, thus
challenged, would 'make themselves air'. This proving to
be mere fancy, we may indeed remark with restrained
applause that a number of those who were famous for their
being so largely the battalion are in the land of the living
yet. There is G.H.H., to begin with; and we could almost
eat him, but a divinity round our Colonel prevents the
instinctive cannibalism from doing what it would. 'Doesn't
look a day older,' whispers sergeant to sergeant – no, Mr
Davey, DCM, to Mr Worley, DCM – as G.H.H. rises to
address us, and professes that when he received orders to
quit his original Regiment and come to us, above all when
he first saw us, he was filled with wrath and – 'well, I won't
tell you what I did think,' with a twinkling eye. He then tells
us how he grew to delight in commanding us – and a (still
sober) voice fills a pause, 'And you weren't … so bad.'
Memories of the Somme will follow, and, as G.H.H. is a
soldier by descent and character, when he has blessed us for
sitting so patiently in the mudholes of the Schwaben
Redoubt he blesses us even more vividly for marching in to
Doullens, singing our song, not a 'column of lumps' but –
the battalion. What makes the appearance of G.H.H.
among us so completely appropriate and remindful is the

fact that on his right, with his mallet of office in his hand, sits J.L., his adjutant, our wisest, heartiest, safest guide – under G.H.H. – now as in 1916. When J.L. speaks, hesitation, melancholy, dispute are impossible; good sense and manhood seem our natural and inseparable qualities. He, too, appears to us very little altered from the days when, watching all and worrying none, he rode his horse over the training-ground behind Arras, or when he sat in that stifling glum cave beyond Hamel with the Colonel, ignoring the blasts of high explosive at the gaping entrance, trying to hold a crazy attack in its proper place.

We have C.M. too, and who could fail to recognize him still, at the other end of the hall? He was an integral part of *my* battalion which, as I confessed, slipped away from me. I recall the admiration I felt at his mighty throwing of bombs, and his going ahead of us to Thiepval when that poor place was still being gunned and bombed and bayonetted and gassed for the lease. He has a spirit which I envy, for, in part freeing himself from this incubus-like inspiration of ours, he studies what men were before the calamity, and what they are now and under what conditions. His speech is not over-reminiscent, but gay, comfortable, a little risky. He, indeed, makes us a little uneasy about our recurrence to the bitter past, the rhapsodical touch in our reason for being here. Are we becoming romantic? G.M. here is not; he always was. Rosy youth never deserted him, with all its glowing sensibilities. He dramatized, or enjoyed the dramatic in, the dreariest situations of the grey old confusion. He was one of the few who would speak of God without the purposes of exasperation, as a sublime, inscrutable and natural Being even above the swilling mudpools of Spoil Bank. His finest gesture we take to have been in the greasy but protective tunnels of Canada Street – the one shelter between Gheluvelt and Ypres then; having just performed a damnable miracle in delivering certain supplies at a gas-filled and thunderous spot called a Copse, he reported 'completion' to the General. The General turned from his plank table and guttering candles, and, finding that G.M. had no receipt for the supplies, became excited, harangued, sent him off to get one in that ghoulish night. G.M. went, found another human being at the Copse, obtained the receipt, returned to the General, saluted in his finest manner as he submitted the paper, and withdrawing in perfect silence saluted again. And this fantasy or faith we find still when G.M. comes in among us. He should do it on horseback! but his conversation is as blithe as that would be.

So far I have been speaking of those who were our officers – I have chosen one or two, from whose examples you are to understand the whole number; and that I do so and accord them precedency is not forced. It is in the order of our reunion. The 'other ranks', the 'NCO's and men', at least on such occasions preserve their battalion's spirit as they knew it, not unceremoniously; their officers must be officers still, men of trust, commissioned after all by the King, honourable and fine. I have seen many varieties of beautiful simplicity in my life. The ancient Japanese farmer, making me at home on his rough and ready *tatami*, a trifle hard up for topics, suddenly remembered a means of coming nearer: what a smile of delight he had when he said, 'your country and mine were allies in the War, weren't they?' The childless wife, talking softly to the nesting blackbird that knew her, was a picture of beauty. With such treasures I count the voluntary, sweet and accomplished courtesy which I see in our reunions from the men to the officers – and from them again, in another and equally valuable sense, to the men.

How, one asks again, did some of these 'other ranks' come through? C.A.U., for example, without whom half of us perhaps might not have heard of these evenings, went through fire and water indescribable; not only has he come through, he is radiant with a mastery of life. This is the kind of man who is jostled in the street by many who would have fallen to pieces with a tithe of his burdens in Flanders; the fact never occurs to him, and he would think it not worth the note of indignation. Order and cheerfulness go where he goes, the rations are served out, the complainants treated to a quick epigram on their size in jaws, stomachs and opinions, and he is visiting the listening-posts in the rat-haunted crater. With him is quiet J.C., whom nobody ever offended or felt a wish to offend – his fortunate company depended on his thoughtful unerring work for years. A.D. and F.W. are together – that friendship was famous! Their shyness has not passed away; perhaps it has even increased. Of these two men, too much was demanded; have I not been guilty of that myself, not noticing that even they could feel the last straw? W.A.C. comes over to give a hint or two for the speeches. I doubt whether he slept on the average three hours a day and night in 1916 and 1917. I remember his pale face (I wished a great painter might have seen him as I did) when, in a dead midnight, he looked up from the mass of papers by which the battalion partly retained its right to exist. A mystic might have had that look; and I can interpret – C. had for the battalion that kind of constant perceiving love which denies all self-concern. Once he and I had a swamp to cross, tree-stump by tree-stump; our predecessors there were there still – very still – for there was a ferocious shelling in it. He was laughing to me as we set out – and here we are, and he is attributing what I praise in him to 'mainly Memory' – the calm ambiguous rogue! – and saying, 'I can give you some stories about Avard.' Now T.Y. ventures to claim a word; him too I remember mainly at night, with the signallers' headphones on, doing his best with the squeaky buzzer, going on for ever if need be. That loud and frequent cry 'Basso' sounds across our talk and the noise of the assembly; Basso is used to it; he is a hospitable humorist, apparently unaltered since the Western Front. When it comes, as it must, to my making a speech, you will see one listener particularly anxious and, if we have luck, particularly applauding, from the far end of the room; that tall youth with the shining ruddy cheek and the golden hair. H.T.N. was a runner, and few runners ever failed in their solitary courage; he excelled. His friend, H., of his own calibre, should be here; H.T.N. is just a shade disconsolate, but his smiling face can never be darkened.

The rest of them? I could name many, and – here is that old dilemma – many I could not. They came, probably, when I began to be retrospective, in the very midst of our war history, over the battalion; when the hurry, and hope-lessness, and a new selfishness, reduced my powers of becoming acquainted. Now and then, they will overcome diffidence and give me a clue which leads back to a scene that had been concealed. It is a pity that S.J.S. is not here this evening; he is the infallible index to everyone, and everything – the walking log-book of the battalion. But for me, who am to address the party, it may be as well that he is prevented; one slip over a name or a date, and he 'could throw a plate at you'. But error is one thing, legend another. I find in some of us an innocent formation of legends in process – a natural outgrowth from our longing to keep in view the battalion we served with as, in its way, 'a glorious birth'. G.H.H. himself ascribes to me, and has described to the assembled host, a far from attractive patrol in the marshes east of Hamel Mill; he asseverates – no slighter term will do – that I announced to him my intention of the patrol and of writing a poem on the Mill, and that I accom-plished both. Possibly I told him of the patrol afterwards with poetic licence; at all events, he is as sure of it as of the poem, which I actually produced to him. Then, my dear E.F., to whom I owed many of my first sensible movements in the region of Festubert and La Bassée Canal, has been pressing me to agree with his reminiscences of an adven-ture, on the night when Beaumont Hamel was being taken (be grateful, you absentees!) which betrayed young Johnson and myself a long way into the German zone. How approv-ingly should I have seen E.F. with us; but, though he declares he was, and that it was he who repeatedly informed me that we were well on the way to Berlin, I am telling you, – not him – that he was not. He joined us after-wards, at the south-east corner of Thiepval Wood; and had the high-velocity shells fallen a few yards otherwise just then there would have been no chance of my thus asserting the grace of accurate history. But am I right? Is it grace? I grow shadowy myself, and next year I shall be liable to substantiate E.F.'s projections in every letter.

These oddities I mention as being within my own area; but the evening advances, the speeches and the music are drawing to an end – all but my speech, which J.L. has placed last on the bill. He replies, to my protest, that at that stage nobody will take any notice of what is actually said; the battalion is not teetotal yet; the beer is not the 'bière speciale pour Cantines' which we inhaled at Poperinghe. Many seats, in front of the tables decorated with our blue and orange colours, are empty now, and their occupants are heartily exchanging recollections and liquids at the business side of the restaurant. Tankards and tumblers are gently set down before us, and – may I boast of it unblamed? – a hand or two ruffles my hair, a voice or two says 'Don't you wish it was the old Eleventh?' and 'There, my dear, you're a good old boy.' The old Eleventh! I shall be speaking to them – to these who would, at need, give up everything this hour to follow G.H.H. again in some rare enterprise, even to be 'crimed' by G.M. for dirty harness and led by me into some absurd predicament; but not only to them. Were I a maker of tragic spectacle, I could fill some of those vacated seats with forms as piteous as Banquo's. There is no need for that, no need for vacant places; those to whom I would also be audible, and by whose judgment I am content to stand or fall, are present to most of our minds. The great Essayist who declined, even in his illustrious Elian wit – melancholy, to put himself on paper, once called on his schoolfellow Coleridge to re-possess his vision: 'Come back into memory, like as thou wert in the day-spring of thy fancies.' We could use the phrase, and the feeling is ours; for we have never permitted ourselves to think of our best men as the mangled victims of the vile machinery that ended their toil. They come back alive, hale, genial, ready to be anything in the hope of being ever.

Come, Daniels. G.H.H. was at one time inclined to be

your severe critic. He 'has heard more since', and you know how he loved you after all. Here is Worley – you remember how you discovered in him the original of Bairnsfather's 'Old Bill'. Had I but dreamed you would soon be – but you were always a humanist. There are no bags of Very Lights now for you to send up to the company headquarters, no parade states; be free. If you will, we will be on parade at six; but now relax, and see around you what you were to us. And Ashford, you are not likely to be far off on such a night. There is no champagne going – you have forgotten? I haven't; it was you who introduced me in your best manner to that wine. It was one summer evening, dusky-brilliant, and I was emerging from a talk about next day's training programme with C. in his office, in the labourer's cottage at Houlle. Moulle! Houlle. Ah, well,

*How delightfully we would go*
    *To Houlle and Moulle*
    *And the bathing-pool*
*And the –*

Preparations for the show? But, about that Heidsieck, I was emerging, it was hard to see for a moment, and there was a voice, your voice, and a hand, your hand, and a bottle, your bottle; and on the whole I liked champagne. Next morning I said I didn't? But there were later tests. I wish you would tell me – did you ever feel fear? I never noticed it. I saw you melancholy once, without a smile – it was when I came to say I was for England. You had a prescient gift, I thought, and not only then. This is Clifford. Easiest of friendships, ours; how imperceptibly we drew together, until if I was on the duckboards towards Hill 60 I could be pretty sure the man following me was you. We hardly had our fair share of walks and gossip in peaceful places – I see you almost inevitably with a slab of muddy sandbags behind you, and your telescope under your arm. You even recall my giving you my field-glasses? Well, you were very flattering about them, and then, you did something with them. It all sounds dreamy now, absurd almost; how your eye shone as you described the German trolley-pushing party that you were observing towards Comines! You would not have changed places then with Rockefeller, I think you said. Calm as a country Sunday you moved through your last labours. Blue-eyed and fair, reasonable and – but it is no courtesy to praise a man to his face. Anyway, put those field-glasses under the table. Tice! our own Prussian! The Prussians are not now regarded as they were, journalistically, when you were in the dugout on Canal Bank. No, my dear, we did not *mean* that you were a caricature Prussian in grain! I am ashamed to have lost the address of that excellent widow-woman near Zuytpeene who was so proud of having so gentle, so wise, so saintly a being under her roof as Tice; and what a dinner she put up for us, your friends. I liked the letter she wrote you better than the story of Ruth; I wrote to her after July 31st. If I think of Clifford with a pair of binoculars I think of you with a map-case and a compass; throw them away, you old non-sleeper, and listen to what Collyer there is saying. He is surely not talking of Pozières? He is, and thanks to our army training, we know he is although he refers to it as Jammy Whiskers. Vidler interrupts with a tale he heard in Vancouver, no, it is simply his imitation of a Chinese laundry-boy, followed by – O Vid, we know it by heart, *par coeur*, well, 'It's like this here, sir, not feeling quite meself this morning, sir, I eats all right and I sleeps all right, but …'

At our last feast, there was one with us whom we could not imagine ever being away. He is away, this year, and except under the dispensation which has just permitted me to fill up some of the empty chairs with my lost companions, he will be away throughout the series now. Regimental Sergeant-Major Ball was what is called a 'character', and a little perturbed and suspicious about his being regarded as such. Perhaps that was the only reason why he was now and then subdued. But what should he do about it? After all – and then he would release the full benefit of his personality and colloquial zest. With a short explosion of a laugh he would drive home his point. 'And you remember them fellows I brought in out of no-man's-land, and brought into that water-store where you was? And you remember how blasted dry we all were and so were you, and there didn't seem to be anything for it except drink that water? But – there was something else. I hadn't got my water-bottle on for nothing, had I? You remember? IT CAME UP RUM!' Of course it did. Ball had a lusty spirit, a loud indignant geniality, which made anything less than rum impossible even in a smashed water-store on the edge of a murderous and groaning no-man's-land. A singer, too, at battalion gaffes. Once he 'came on', at such a concert in a capital big hutment far from enemies, just after a turn by two mischievous young accomplices who had mimicked with deplorable accuracy the gestures and the conversation of – Ball. Either he had not quite detected that or he had decided to triumph by sheer and complete agreement and superior demonstration; for he strode the platform full of his grand manner – to say, I again suggest, that

*None but himself could be his parallel.*

Eyeing the house as he would eye a squad of defaulters, he opened his mouth to give us a most monotonous ballad of which he produced the words with impressive emphasis – so much so, that after fifteen years I remember them, or some of them.

*Once I went to a Res-taw-rong*
*With an appetite about* Twelve yards long;
*Ordered poultry* [here he shrugged his shoulders], *up it* came.
*When it got there, it was* GAME;
*A sort of a* tarry twang *arose*
*As soon as I touched it on the* nose ...
     *Postponed,*
     *Me Dinner,*
          *&c.*

As he sang, there grew an imperfectly repressed murmur of delight from front to back of the hall; Ball seemed aware of it, and, like the traveller in Mr. de la Mare's haunted forest, he expressed himself 'even louder', and rolled on triumphantly to the final stanza and its 'Postponed – The Wedding'.

Ball, in spite of the apparent impossibility, is dead and gone; I mentioned his occasionally lapsing into a subdued manner. Now, for all the jubilation, commotion, talk, speechifying and chorusing in the room tonight, a subdued manner may be perceived in the individuals, and if we could investigate it without these agreeable interruptions (signing menus on these occasions has to be done, in Keats's words, with 'a fine excess') we might again discover 'the battalion'. On the whole, as G.H.H. remarked with such parental pleasure, the Peace has not treated our lucky lads too harshly in matters of common prosperity; they seem, most of them, to be holding their own with necessity, even if we allow that some absentees were kept away by poverty. Not thence comes the subdued manner. But, if I may diagnose, these are for ever a shade different from those who missed their former experiences. They are accustomed to looking into those memories which would not often be welcome talk to their neighbours. They see the works of the Lord, but his wonders in the deep are past; those too they saw. The mystery of that, the misery and the dignity reside for them in the word, 'the battalion'. The future cannot rival that attraction. They, we, are years behind even the present, and minor reservations and limitations of date, place and contact yield to one strong retrospective migratory devotion. But J.L. is hammering again to warn us of a speech, and I am the machine that must make it. I am less sure of my past and present than I pretended to be when we sat down. Will there be chairs enough for all of us, as the troops return to the tables to listen forgivingly to this rhetoric? At what point do we separate from those other listeners I named? Are we not all in the same boat? Fall in, ghosts.

*Note*

The preceding impression is actually derived from an annual dinner
attended not by one battalion, but by three, which were raised and
brigaded together and shared the same career in France and Belgium.
For my purpose I have only alluded to members of my own unit, with
hardly an exception; were I writing at greater length, this would not have
been the case; but my purpose was to typify. This explanation is due to
my friends of the 12th and 13th Battalions, if any of them should chance
to see my essay; their part in the whole is not excluded for any reason
but that of the simplicity demanded by my writing limits.

Published as a pamphlet (1932). Reprinted in *Contemporary Essays*, edited
by Sylva Norman (London, 1933); collected in *The Mind's Eye* (London,
1934).

# A BATTALION HISTORY

(with apologies)

The Southdown Battalions' Association dines annually at the Brighton Aquarium, doubtless startling the regular inhabitants with its boisterous cheerfulness. At the last dinner something occurred which also startled me. It was publicly proposed, and so far as I could observe it was generally demanded, that I should write the history of one at least of these Southdown Battalions. In a spirit of mingled cowardice and devotion to duty I found myself rising to accept this 'onerous honour' (the evening was far advanced); and I now present my old friends with something which nominally tallies with their request. Unfortunately it is shorter than they expected, but the war was also shorter than they expected.

The 11th Royal Sussex Regiment, otherwise the First Southdowns, otherwise Lowther's Lambs (and of course the Iron Regiment), being composed principally of Sussex men, was formed at the outset of the war, but was not sent overseas until March, 1916. On March 5th the battalion landed at Havre. A week later, in the usual fashion of that period, it left billets in Morbecque for trenches at Fleurbaix, in which it received instruction from the Yorks and Lancs. The first casualty (a man killed by a bullet) happened in the communication trench on the way in. Within a year, those who could speak from experience of Fleurbaix, the convent wall, and the suspect farmer ploughing in view of the Germans with white or black horses on different occasions, were rare. The day after the debut, possibly because of too conspicuous parades, some company billets in Fleurbaix were suddenly shelled with accuracy and the battalion lost sixteen men killed and wounded.

By March 20th the battalion, its rapid probation over, held a trench subsector by itself; after its four days there it emerged through quiet Estaires to Merville, then undamaged, and spent three weeks under training there. 'Training' made a considerable part of the war's burden. The battalion next marched through the plain southward to Hingette, a hamlet on the canal west of Béthune, well away from the trenches except for some primitive ones that intersected the fields, intended to be ready for some strange upheaval. An eastward move soon followed; billets at Gorre were quitted on April 19th and muddy trenches at Givenchy were taken over. Here the side-effects of the quarrels south of the Canal, in the grim contorted country by Loos, were felt and paid for in some casualties. May-day arrived, and that night the battalion was relieved. Among the willow-shaded lanes of Hinges by the Canal beyond Béthune, it passed several days; much cleaning-up, much *parlez-vousing*, and on one evening at least, the Band playing. Thence it marched away on May 9th to le Touret, in the rain, and from that straggling hamlet it supplied working-parties until on the 14th it relieved the 13th Royal Sussex in the moonlight along the breastworks of Festubert. A famous name! but May, 1916, was anything but the repetition of that dreadful one of the previous year, which had sown the marshy grounds we dug in with skulls and equipment. In this Festubert locality of snipers and machine-guns we manned our posts and patrolled and wired for almost a fortnight, and when the Hertfordshires had relieved us we returned hopefully to the Hingette cottages and lofts.

But suddenly on May 28th, amid fearsome rumours, the battalion was ordered up to the front line south of the La Bassée Canal, at Cuinchy, which was a 'hot shop'. Here it was that the first Military Cross was awarded to one of us (Lieut. H.S. Lewis), followed by the first Military Medals (to G. Compton and W. Booth); the action concerned had occurred in no-man's-land at Givenchy. The business of the trenches at Cuinchy was strenuous; heavy trench

mortars fired often into us, and on June 3rd the Germans
sent out a fighting patrol which only succeeded in bombing
a few posts. Next night a mine was blown just ahead of our
front trench; in spite of the miscalculation, the explosion
and the savage shelling that immediately lit up the wet
darkness cost us six killed and thirty-seven wounded. The
battalion might have suffered even worse casualties had an
unprepared raid on the fortifications opposite (which was
to have been made by us) been attempted; but it is understood that Colonel Grisewood, at the price of being
removed from his command, rescued us from this
menacing plan. From the Cuinchy trenches we were withdrawn for the usual short rest at Annequin, a village of
colliers and pigeons, and we came back early on June 8th
in small parties. This front-line tour produced two more
mines, one German, one (the more imposing) ours; these
did us no harm; some bombing matches took place where
the two trench systems almost joined. We were now
promoted to the dignity of instructing the 8th Warwicks.
During the night of the 11th an Argyll and Sutherland
battalion took our place and we very wearily returned to
Hingette.

North and south of the La Bassée canal were, and are,
when you know them, different countries. We next went
north again into the agricultural country, lay west of Neuve
Chapelle for several days and at night were busy with picks,
shovels and trench carpentering towards Richebourg
l'Avoué. At midnight on June 21st we were relieving the
12th ('Second') Battalion about Ferme du Bois, and in
those breastworks and muddy ditches we remained until
the 28th, when by daylight the Cambridgeshires came
cheerfully in to relieve us and we were scattered in detach-
ments among the keeps of Richebourg St Vaast. Major
G.H. Harrison about now succeeded to Colonel Grisewood, and for a time he had the continued services of
Captain Wallace – a splendid soldier – as adjutant. Meanwhile, we were informed of the opening of the Great
Offensive of 1916, and of a local share in it. Down the

road, a canvas representation of a projecting corner of the
German parapet, known as the Boar's Head, was rigged
up, and our storm-troops were practised at it. The Boar's
Head was to be bitten off on June 30th, mainly by the other
battalions of our 116th Brigade; but from our battalion
large parties were detailed for carrying and some bombing.
We knew little of the aims of this attack, and in our view it
appeared a much greater thing than it in fact was. It seems
to have been intended to delay some German troops and
artillery from their march south to the Sommeschlacht.
The attack was advertised by a preliminary bombardment
from our batteries on the afternoon of June 29th. We
looked across at the flying woodwork and earthwork of the
German line. On the next morning, while it was still dark,
both artillery groups let fly (ours had a few seconds' start),
and our infantry went over. The German machine-guns
had no difficulty; the Brigade and the supporting pioneers
and Engineers were massacred, our own casualties being
one hundred and twenty killed, wounded and missing.
Among the survivors were some, such as G. Compton, who
had gone deep into the German lines almost alone.

Next afternoon, while this kind of thing was being
enacted through miles and miles of Picardy, we were
relieved and came to Lacouture, or the orchards that
fringed it. We lived partly in light huts and the hours were
punctuated by the fire of the heavies. On July 6th at night
we were surprised to find ourselves marching south (and
incidentally breathing tear-gas). We slept briefly at Beuvry
(then a place that pleased us much), but next day advanced
through the pale rain, in parties of six, along the stone
highway east. The 4th King's Liverpools willingly made
room for us in the trenches before Auchy, which were
seldom free for an hour from the stinging blasts of all sorts
of bombs and shells. Our casualties were all too many. This
strain on the nerves lasted a week or so, and we were glad
to be sent up to le Touret once more. On July 20th we held
the Ferme du Bois line again, and on the 23rd a raiding
party was sent across, but its failure cost us seven killed and

wounded. Next day we side-stepped into the Festubert breastworks, and held them in high summer weather, when even the War took a siesta, until the 29th. It was daring to try a relief here in broad day but it came off, and we assembled after it at le Touret among the chicken-runs and estaminets. Then, to the general rejoicing, several days of billets in Béthune were given us. The people were kind and the food was cheap. Some may have visited the Red Lamp area, but not so many as would do in many War Books. After this holiday we occupied the trenches at Givenchy again, and made good use of the sunshine and the canal by bathing in the afternoons, about 200 yards from the nearest Germans. Some of these tried to fraternize one morning. Their opening joke was an allusion to bully beef and biscuits; but at that time we were well fed even in the trenches. On August 11th we left Givenchy for what had been long foretold – our part in the Battle of the Somme.

The period thus concluded was quite a distinct one. Throughout the battalion was seldom at any distance from the trenches – but the trenches were in the main 'truly rural'. Horrible and destructive moments occurred, yet there was something of beauty and of health in the general impression. You soon came into the scenes of ordinary life as you left the front line behind. The ruins of Richebourg St Vaast, of Festubert and even of Cuinchy and Givenchy were substantial, and bits of architecture, gardens and plats attracted us even beyond warning notice-boards about 'daylight movement'. We were now to become acquainted with a mood of War which permitted no half-measures and no estaminets on the communication trench.

Marching well west of the battlefield, we saw unusual sights such as the aerodrome near Auchel, and I think a military mineral-water works before that. We were in high spirits, knowing nothing of the actualities we were making for. On the 13th we reached Monchy Breton, a dank village in the Arras area, out of which we marched for training on some breezy downs chequered with thick woods. Here was ground said to be just like that we were to attack in reality.

Minute instructions were given, and followed by all ranks. Early on the 24th we were on the road again, and our march was assisted by a short train journey; the night we spent at le Souich ('Oh, *swish*'), and six hours dusty tramp next day brought us to Warnimont Wood at two in the afternoon. Reconnaissances at a front-line village called Hamel, on the River Ancre, detached some parties on the 26th and 27th, when all moved to P.18 or Mailly-Maillet Wood – a dishevelled little scrubbery viewed by German observation balloons and shelled unpleasantly. The battalion transport shared the wood and suffered from the shelling. After making its forward preparations, hindered by much rain, and after two postponements of the attack, the battalion filed into its assembly trenches on Hamel hillside by midnight of September 2nd. At 5. 10 on the 3rd the attack began. The gunfire was heavier than we had known. I believe no one can say what happened to our bombing parties under young Lieut. French, who was to clear up the suspected German dugouts in the railway cutting. Nor is there much detail of our main waves. Led by Captain Northcote, a number of men went past the German front trenches, and formed an isolated post. The majority, under Captain Michell and 2nd Lieut. James Cassels, dug in nearer the German parapet. Nothing could be done to relieve the attack, which had collapsed north and south as well. The order to withdraw was sent in the afternoon but Northcote and his valiant companions were not successful in their attempt to re-cross no-man's-land. The battalion (relieved by the Cheshires) assembled in a trench along Hamel village street and in the setting sun arrived at Englebelmer, three hundred fewer in number than when it passed through that village the evening before. Temporary organization in two companies instead of four was found necessary. The survivors seemed scarcely to realize their survival; it was a dizzy end to an incredible day.

On the 6th we moved, no great distance, to Beaussart, where there were a few civilians whom the men distrusted. Reinforcements from England – four hundred men – were

received here. Colonel Harrison rapidly restored the
battalion to its normal working. On the morning of the
14th we took over the extensive trenches before Beaumont
Hamel and once in appeared unlikely ever to get out.
However we were for the present secure from the painful
chaos of fighting a few miles south. In these trenches
(supported by the decaying positions of Auchonvillers) we
worked hard and were shelled and trench-mortared not too
violently most days; but the minenwerfers caused casualties. Gas-shelling on September 23rd may be noted; at that
date, the only box-respirator in the battalion was at headquarters. To assist the troops in the attacks on Thiepval,
southward, we put up rows of dummies in screens of
smoke. On October 4th under a burst of shelling we were
relieved, but only in order that we might make a circuit
through Englebelmer Wood and Martinsart Wood on our
way to the Hamel trenches. A party was sent up during this
short interval to reconnoitre the region of Thiepval Wood,
which was at that time intensely contested. Hamel was
better. Moonlight nights threw a strange illusion over the
Ancre valley, and autumn afternoons glowed among the
wildflowers along our communication trench, Jacob's
Ladder, which began at the poisonous spot Mesnil. The
battalion occupied a front usually held by two battalions,
and did this safely for ten days. A smoke barrage was
produced by us and the trench mortars on October 12th to
call off German attention from an attack south of the river.
The Royal Naval Division relieved us on the 16th, but we
immediately moved into Authuille Wood south of Thiepval
and prepared for an attack. When the battalion occupied
its assembly positions in the frosty muddy upland, on the
20th, it had been roughly five weeks without rest, and was
greatly exhausted; nevertheless, at zero hour (12.7 p.m.,
October 21st) it advanced over the open with beautiful
steadiness to seize Stuff Trench. It did what it was ordered
to do, and held the trench until relief at midnight on the
22nd. The cost was two hundred and seventy-nine killed,
wounded and missing. Among the killed was an especially

cheerful and determined officer named Doogan. The state
of the ground traversed by the battalion was extraordinary,
and the mud-pools were strewn with corpses.

After the relief, some poor tents south of Aveluy Wood
seemed remarkably comfortable; but on the 25th the
battalion was holding the line again (Thiepval Wood), and
thereabouts it stayed, digging and carrying and being
shelled, until the 30th. That morning it worked its way
through heavy rain and a slough of despond past Thiepval
village to Schwaben Redoubt. Here there was always some
shelling, but on the 31st we were systematically bombarded, and when we were relieved (next day) the tour had
cost us thirty-two casualties. The relief was expensive
mostly to the Cheshires, whom the Germans saw coming
in; the business, though simple itself, took five hours. We
rested in the cabin-like dugouts called Authuille Bluffs, on
the steep rise from the Ancre inundations, and then did
even better by getting back as far as Senlis. Two days, and
we were at Thiepval Wood afresh, but quickly returned to
Senlis and its barns and estaminets; on November 7th we
were working in a winter storm in the Aveluy region, and
on the 10th we resumed or were resumed by the Schwaben
Redoubt, which was by now a few deep dugouts and a
maze of crushed and choked trenches. We attempted a raid
the night following, and by good luck caught two German
soldiers without losing anybody. It was beyond the understanding of the men in the mud that an attack by us was
imminent, but that was the fact, and on November 13th
other units of our Division passed through our positions
and overran, or overwaded, the German forts beyond. Our
task should have been the melancholy one of carrying and
dumping wire for the Division in front of its extreme
advance, but there was such a blaze of shells bursting in no-
man's-land in such a vile November night that we were let
off and had to go no further with the materials than the old
front line. This was the close of the battalion's Somme
battle. One night at Pioneer road (huts along a sunk track),
one at Warloy-Baillon (unspoiled houses with curtains and

door-knockers), and then on the 15th a march of fifteen miles ending at Doullens. A train journey north, on November 17th–18th, removed us from the Somme area.

There one may define the end of the second part of this short history. During almost three months the battalion had been practically always under fire, had held trenches for scarcely tolerable periods and shared in three bewildering and devastating attacks. It had been cut off, with little exception, from common sights and scenes of life, and had become accustomed to two views of the universe: the glue-like formless mortifying wilderness of the crater zone above, and below, fusty, clay-smeared, candle-lit wooden galleries, where the dead lay decomposing under knocked-in entrances. The battalion had vastly changed in its personal composition under these prolonged tribulations; of the four hundred men who joined at Beaussart even, a great number were dead, wounded or otherwise vanished before we left the district.

In piercing cold the battalion occupied M Camp among Belgian farms and the huts of refugees, on the Poperinghe-Watou road, and refitted and drilled there until December 5th. When we left M Camp, it was not to try our fate at Ypres as we might have surmised but to find out still quieter places than Poperinghe. We went by train to St Omer and by road to Moulle, near which place we built rifle-ranges. On December 15th, however, there was a train journey ending at the ruins of the Asylum, Ypres, and a turn in the trenches north of that city – Canal Bank. This period was one of the most peaceful and harmless that we ever had in the Line. On the 23rd we were sent back to E Camp in Elverdinghe Woods, and a snowy and joyful Christmas followed, in spite of the reconnaissances that day in the trenches of Boesinghe. There we relieved the 10th South Wales Borderers on the 30th, and the year 1916 ended for us in a dull commonplace trench day.

The Belgian Army were on our left flank at Boesinghe, where the front trench was cut in the raised Canal bank. So was the German trench over the frozen shallow Canal.

Behind us was shapely clean country, and Elverdinghe Château was intact. We were encamped in its neighbourhood for almost a fortnight before a new and memorable experience – a first night in Ypres, to which we came after dark. Some were in the cellars of the Convent, others in basements near the old Station square. Next night we went through the Menin Gate to relieve trenches at Potijze; fierce cold prevailed and heavy snowfall. After four days 'in', we were relieved by our friends the 14th Hants, and sheltered in the same smoky recesses of Ypres, and went in and out for wiring and other work. Eastward again on the 24th – and we had hardly relieved the Hants and settled down to freeze in peace when a box barrage of minenwerfer shells and whizzbangs cut out our extreme right (a strong bombing post). The Germans had thought out a clever raid; their raiders apparently huddled in a culvert, under the railway by which our post was placed, until the moment of entry. Our men (it was evident later) fought hard, but we lost three missing, five killed, others wounded; three of the raiders were killed. The following evening a false gas alarm called down a bitter bombardment, and the next evening another false alarm produced a similar clash. There was great unrest, and we did our best to scour no-man's-land at night; and it was earnest winter weather. The guns and planes were restless as we. The 14th Hants succeeded us on the 28th, and we clanked down the road into Ypres, for more fatigues in the snow. The Germans raided the Hants next, and though we passed a further spell of Potijze (February 1st–4th) without such shocks, after we had gone out by train from Ypres to Vlamertinghe we still provided supporting companies in Potijze village, and reconnoitred emergency and alternative routes over open land to the front trenches. A German attack was apparently feared.

The Vlamertinghe camp was useful for battalion drill (where a hop garden had been), and vast quantities of fuel were burned there; on February 16th we entrained at the Cheesemarket, Poperinghe, on a little railway which took

us to Bollezeele. Great cheerfulness ensued, and the winter
relented at last; but such times sped by, and on the 24th we
were at Winnipeg Camp, Ouderdom, on our way into the
Salient again. Next day we moved to Ypres and Zillebeke
Lake, a reservoir in the Bund on which were dozens of
flimsy dugouts. Headquarters was a tall drab house at
Kruisstraat, memorable to us as the last headquarters of
Colonel Harrison while he was with us. Here he received
an order to proceed to a Staff school in England. Almost at
once the battalion suffered more troubles. The adjutant,
Captain Lintott – brilliant in the Somme battle – was
compelled by illness to leave us. Then when the battalion,
after a terrific struggle through the dark and storm, occupied trenches on Observatory Ridge, it was bombarded
and raided, and lost sixteen killed and wounded. Among
the casualties was the regimental sergeant major, Daniels;
a shell burst in headquarters at Valley Cottages during the
relief, and he died a few days later at Vlamertinghe. A great
man.

Leaving Observatory Ridge, its bony stumps of trees
and naked tracks, on March 3rd, the battalion was some
days in Winnipeg Camp, and reconnoitred a reserve system
at Dickebusch. It returned to Ypres by train but on nearing
the town waited for a furious bombardment to slacken;
once again it took over the Observatory Ridge trenches
from the 14th Hants, amid bursts of rain and gunnery. Four
days on the grill here, then four with night work at Kruisstraat, then Winnipeg Camp again, then the short train
ride and the halt while Ypres was being further pulverized,
and Observatory Ridge once more. This time the four days
ended with the headquarters being driven out of Valley
Cottages (a most dangerous solitary set of ruins) by the
German gunners, and trying to find some better hole in the
scarcely preferable raggedness of Zillebeke. This search the
14th Hants continued, during the night of March 31st; the
battalion retreated into Zillebeke Bund. The snow reap-
peared, and betrayed the secret entrances to the dugouts of
Observatory Ridge, where the battalion again took charge

for four days. Emerging on April 7th, we found an alluring 'revue' being played by the 49th Divisional Follies in a vast hut at Brandhoek, but as we drifted forth from it into the crystal light of evening we saw and heard a display of artillery in the St Eloi direction which 'beat all'. Trouble was anticipated for us, and indeed for everyone in the region; but the German attack was limited and local. There were days in the Infantry Barracks at Ypres (stiff with big guns now); at Brandhoek again, among the farmers; and then in the wet the battalion manned trenches about Hill Top Farm north of Ypres. From these it moved back to the Canal Bank, then a sort of Garden City of pretty dugouts and many of them. The end of April approached, and another Allied Offensive was also thought to be approaching. We entrained at Ypres, passed through our old M Camp, entrained again on May-day and formed up outside St Omer's distinguished-looking station. Marching on (with one night at Hallines), we found very humble billets in a cow-scented village named Zudausques, and were kept miserably and ironically busy with training in a new method of attack. In this manner May, 1917, went by; but halfway through we were transferred to Wormhoudt, where there is a hotel; but we saw little of it. Inspected and trained to a degree, we next moved by road to D camp in the woods of Elverdinghe.

The Salient was becoming uglier all round. The battalion was helping to build railways for a few days, then held trenches – June 1st–6th – at Hill Top. At all hours spiteful bombardments were put down, and the first day brought fourteen casualties. There was gas on all sides, too, when the battalion came back to the Canal Bank; it was no sort of rest, and the next trench tour in a heat-wave had countless grim moments. No place was safe. Those trenches were not made for this power of artillery. On June 16th there was a midnight move to Elverdinghe, and on the 21st we went by train from Poperinghe station (listening to the explosions of shells in the station yard) to Watten and on foot from that dreamy village to even dreamier Houlle.

This move was one of the wetter ones. At Houlle we were happy, beating down much promising corn with our practice offensive, swimming in the big ballast-holes, and approving the inexhaustible beer of the place. And this lasted three weeks and more before the offensive in question dragged us eastward. We arrived then by train at Poperinghe (passing new sidings, and hospitals!) and marched to C Camp, Elverdinghe. It was changed. Camps shelled, air duels, dumps exploding, new roads, tracks, light lines – these were the disorder of the day.

On July 22nd a patrol sent by us to Hill Top under an inexperienced officer disappeared, complete with maps and papers relating to the attack. Other patrols were sent up on later nights. The Canal Bank was full of gas. There were reports of a German withdrawal, but it was found not to be quite an innocent one. By night on July 28th the battalion marched into its assembly area – trenches old and new at Hill Top. Dreary continuous gunning accompanied us. On July 30th, waiting and preparing, at least seven of us were killed and six wounded. The skies had plenty of rain in them, despite liberal disbursements. On July 31st, at 3.50 a.m., as dark as could be, we attacked the demolished High Command Redoubt. The British barrage was such as numbed our powers of realization; the reply to it was instant, but diffused. The battalion took its objectives, and got busy with a line of shell-holes, shaping out some kind of posts; but the rain set in, and what the careful fire of the German heavies did not do the rain did. It rained all night, and through August 1st; and the German gunners, from their reserve positions, fired on with accurate diligence. By 3 a.m. on August 2nd the battalion had gone forward to relieve the 14th Hants in the Black Line, along the Steenbeek; a formidable day followed. Counter-attacks threatened, and were broken up. The German gunners did their utmost for their infantry, and all our headquarters were destroyed by direct hits. From this bad eternity we were relieved at night by the 17th K.R.R., and found our way to the far side of Canal Bank, a hot meal, and what sleep could be got. The blaze of dumps just behind was hardly noticed next day, and nobody was pleased with the prospect of further trouble in the front line; but we escaped that, and by train and road were sent to School Camp, St Jans ter Biezen, beyond Poperinghe. An estimate of our total casualties in the action was two hundred and seventy-five.

The sun came out, and life improved; moreover, when the battalion decamped, it was to a fresh area, that of Meteren, the pretty spire of which looked along the highway to the Moorish steeple of Bailleul. Here a sort of divisional reunion happened, and the bands of several battalions played in the crowded streets; it was as though the spirit of the preceding year were challenging that of 1917. A move to Dickebusch on August 12th, and reconnaissances, preceded the return to the 1917 spirit of Spoil Bank (Hollebeke). Midnight at once produced shelling and gas, which affected everybody. On the 17th the battalion went forward into the shell-holes, not knowing where the Germans were (and the Germans were as well informed about it). Four days of that, and two at Spoil Bank again where the instantaneous fuse caused some losses; thence to Ridge Wood Camp, shells and showers. On the 27th the battalion relieved the Black Watch at Hollebeke (the operation took over seven hours); the dugouts surprised even us by their stench. A wind arose and dried the shell-holes, which was much appreciated. After this term of four days, relief only meant the homeless wreck of old trenches near Spoil Bank, but that was followed by some better days at Ridge Wood Camp.

In mid-September the battalion held the line at Mount Sorrel, and carried in materials for an attack; was in Divisional Reserve at Voormezeele; did four days' slogging in Larch Wood Tunnels. In that hideous neighbourhood, while some of the headquarters were waiting the word to proceed away from the line, a shell fell in their midst, killing seven of our best men. The names of the next camps which the battalion endured sound odd – Ascot Camp, and

Beggars' Rest. From these withered, draggled places we moved into the true gehenna on the 23rd, and the next evening occupied the front line (no line!) south of the Menin Road. This quarter was called Tower Hamlets. The daytime was burning hot, the night subtly cold, and frantic shelling from 'the Tenbrielen Group' continued. On the night of the 24th a German attack drove in the battalion on our left, but Captain P.L. Clark saved our situation (a habit of his). On the 25th this position fighting continued, and on the 26th our brigade attacked and cleared some ruins of Gheluvelt outskirts. There had never been, in all our experience, such shelling; and the SOS signal went up north and south most monotonously. On the 27th at last one of the shells that hit the headquarters pillbox went through and killed six. How the Rifle Brigade relieved us in daylight, we scarcely knew. We halted a few hundred yards back in Bodmin Copse, and the copse was treated to measured and exact shelling from heavy howitzers. Gas shells came later, but we got away, and that night were carried on lorries from Bus House, St Eloi, to Berthen, hilly and windy country. The casualties of this Menin Road tour were estimated at 200.

Now the usual restlessness of 'rest' ensued, parades, cleanings, baths, exercises, and lastly reconnaissances. Mt. Kokereele was left behind reluctantly on October 15th, and on the way up to the battlefield a shell dropped among headquarters staff with deadly effect. In that district there was hardly time, or condition, for noticing who was dead. Round some deep waterlogged tunnels called Hedge Street and Canada Street this was particularly the case. The battalion spent two nights in the Tunnels, then three in the front line, where once a stream called the Bassevillebeek had flowed. It now lurked in a yellow swamp. The front line was calmer than could have been dreamed, and the tour was lucky. The guns were fighting the guns rather than us. The German artillery ignored an SOS call from their infantry who took our being relieved to be an assembly for attack. We withdrew to Bois Camp, near Dickebusch

Brasserie – a set of melancholy bivouacs; but we got a little warmer on October 21st (the anniversary of our Stuff Trench success) by marching to baths at Kemmel Château. It is not everyone who has a château to bathe in. Two days after that distinction we were transferred to some old horse-lines near Reninghelst, which amounted to an involuntary cold bath; the wind howled and the rain flashed white. Odd jobs followed, and at least we were promoted to the decencies of Chippewa Camp on the 29th. From that place we went forward about October 31st to carry the customary 'materials' and dig a trench beyond Hill 60 – an operation well conducted (Col. Millward's headquarters were in Larch Wood Tunnels, one of the finest works of the kind). There was a lavishing of gas shells and general 'ironware' on our tracks; but on the morning of November 1st we were met by lorries in St Eloi and so 'home'.

The name 'Tower Hamlets' had a pernicious sound for us, but to that point of the firing line the battalion was sent next (Nov. 3rd). Its chief performance was to throw smoke bombs, assisting operations at Polderhock Château just north and Passchendaele farther off. A harmless relief followed, but when the battalion had gone as far back as Bodmin Copse a single shell killed three officers and NCOs (I make no attempt to register all casualties; this is by way of example). On November 7th the battalion moved farther back to Godezonne, *vulgo* God's Own Farm, Vier-straat; and in the succeeding days it went, *via* Chippewa Camp and plenty of rain to Bedford House, a mud-spot near Ypres. For the rest of the year 1917 the 11th Royal Sussex were mainly employed as workmen, under the direction of the Royal Engineers or our own Pioneers. A few days – November 25th to 29th – were granted at Winnizeele, almost civilization; on the 29th the battalion took a train at Godewaerswelde to Ypres. The train made good time, leaving at 8.55 a.m. and covering the dozen or more kilometres by 10 a.m. Encamped on the Potijze Road, the battalion built lengths of railway and causeway; all might have been friendly but for air raids. At 5.30 on the

evening of December 6th, one bomb killed eight and
wounded eight. These men thus missed the agreeable
return from St Jean station (a scarcely believable sign of the
British advance) to Winnizeele and thence to the barns of
Seninghem. There in spite of the eternal training
programme and rifle-range, Christmas was, as they say,
celebrated; on Boxing Day there were snowball fights.

The year 1917 ended with the battalion in Siege Camp,
by Ypres. Siege Camp was left for Morocco Camp, another
bleak place with a view of Passchendaele, of no touristic
value. In rain and snow, from January 16th at dawn to dark
on the 18th, the battalion held a few advanced mudholes at
Westroosebeke. Trench feet (a crime) became a serious
concern. For about a week the battalion remained in Hill
Top Farm, among its memories of old trench tours and the
initial Passchendaele attack, and in School Camp. A big
move was in preparation, and, having entrained at Proven
on January 26th, 1918, the battalion arrived after twelve
hours at Mericourt, in the south of the British line.

Thus ended the battalion's principal connection with
poor Ypres and her sad Salient. It had been a lengthy
connection, and one which we should have wished to end
sooner. It is true that through 1917, when we were not in
the line, we were sent often enough to a considerable
distance from it, and passed weeks in sleepy villages and
safety. Moreover, philanthropy from above frequently
caused one or other of us to be dispatched to one of the
courses of instruction, far from enemies, that multiplied
through this year. But the dreary dreadfulness of front line
experiences now, the sense of a curse over and round Ypres,
the 'looped and ragged nakedness' of forward camps, the
air war on them, the apparent futility of the British effort,
and the shattering of all unity by casualties beyond our
counting, made that year at Ypres a bad business.

Invigorated by the prospect of a new front that, whatever it would be, was not Ypres, we moved forward past
Peronne. By light railway, in a fantastic scene of trees
bearded with hoar frost, and a ghostly silence, we came to

the Cambrai battlefield and the ruins of Gouzeaucourt on a hill. We worked this subsector, between Revelon Farm as close support and the firing-line with its useful deep dugouts and keeps, until March 12th – about thirty-six days; and a great deal of digging, wiring and carrying was done besides the actual maintenance and defence of the positions. Originally calm, the place became noisy and deadly – there were tragedies on the duckboard tracks. On March 9th, crossing the wide no-man's-land, D Company entered the German trenches and found nobody. At last the battalion was taken out, and was busy for a few days finding its way about GHQ Line, in Gurlu Wood and Hem; it was at Hem on March 21st. *Dies Irae.* Then came the Germans. The story hereabouts feels the strain. On the 21st–22nd the battalion was fighting and withdrawing at Villers Faucon, on the 22nd–23rd on a ridge near Bussu, then along the Somme Valley and across the river at Buscourt, and at Hem on the 24th. Reorganization at Chuignolles (March 25th), a withdrawal near Harbonnières (26th), through Harbonnières (28th), a Divisional concentration at Cayeux (noon of the 28th) – these are the dry bones of this episode. Then on March 29th the battalion faced the Germans at Wiencourt, withdrew to Ignaucourt, to a sunk road north of Aubercourt, to another south of Courcelles; on the 30th, it was driven back in the early morning and gradually retreated to the Villers-BretonneuxAubercourt Road. A fine position was taken up before the Bois de Hangard and improved at once; then on the last of March the 18th Division relieved. To collect what remained of the battalion was the next task, at Cléry and Amatre. The action had cost 20 officers, 300 other ranks killed, wounded and missing. On April 7th the unit marched twenty-five kilometres to Embleville and on the 9th entrained for Arques near St. Omer.

But rest was not yet. Ypres even was not done with. A day or two at Tatinghem, and there was a railway journey to Vlamertinghe. Toronto Camp, Otago Camp, and another march to Voormezeele, with its ugly associations.

Here the battalion began a new trench system and had
soon the chance to test it, the Germans (after several days
of cannonading) attacking it early on April 25th. The
shelling of Elzenwalle Château ruins was tremendous, and
it was there that headquarters had placed themselves. On
the 26th the battalion re-took from the Germans its old
friend Dickebusch Brasserie. There were new alarms,
assaults and barrages next day, but the King's Liverpools
relieved that night, and the 11th went into support near
Dickebusch Camp. The noise of battle, and more than
noise, involved it even there, but it had a night or two at
Devonshire Camp. On May-day, the battalion relieved in
the front line. This tour ended on the night of May 3rd, and
so far as I know that was the last time on which the 11th
Royal Sussex as such had any concern with trench tours. By
way of St Jans ter Biezen and M Camp, well known resting-
places, it was withdrawn to Nielles-les-Ardres, near
Audruicq, which again is quite near Calais.

There the battalion was split up. Part of it was given the
honour of instructing American infantry, and afterwards
served in the mysterious campaign in North Russia. Arctic
kit was finally handed in, and the whole history ended.
Ended? Not while the Southdown battalions meet, as
annually they do, to preserve their co-relationships. In
sketching the movements of the 11th Royal Sussex overseas, I have hardly referred to the personalities who most
of all would be mentioned among us when we gather now.
I hardly know how to do it, without doing injustice to many
others on whom, consciously or unconsciously, we relied.
Let me remember Lieut. Swain, our unbeatable quartermaster, and one who was ever with us though not of us, our
Brigade Commander, General Hornby. In my rapid chronicle there is nothing about the life and labours of our
Transport, who never once let us down (we ate our iron
rations at Stuff Trench, but there was some misunder-
standing). Of the impressions we had, of every place and
time we knew, I could not unprompted give a fair general
account now; some we have mercifully forgotten in the

main, others we have a trick of remembering. It is all so long ago now; and yet when I think of the 11th Royal Sussex on a winter evening, under all its ordeals or in any of its recreations,

*Bare winter suddenly is changed to spring.*

Dated 1933 when collected in *The Mind's Eye* (London, 1934), but its earlier publication could not be traced by Blunden's bibliographer, B.J. Kirkpatrick.

# INFANTRYMAN PASSES BY

## I

In the early months of 1914 I was very little concerned with world affairs, except that my mother used sometimes to caution us under the rubric 'when you go out into the world' which we told her meant at the moment the small market town 2 or 3 miles off. The scene of her repeated admonition was the schoolhouse in a very small village in Sussex, in the south of England, within comfortable reach – by bicycle – of the seacoast and above all the enchantments of 'London by the Sea', Brighton. Heroic expeditions to that city with all its huge hotels and piers and fashion parades along the seafront were sometimes managed, but my leadership could only be infrequent and while I was on holiday from my school.

The school was in the same county of Sussex and also inland, about as far away from the sea as our village, and that geographical detail used to matter in one's feelings. It is strange now to think what a distance lay between the schoolhouse and the English Channel in a sense of security (Napoleon having gone away) and equally between Christ's Hospital, Horsham, and those waters. That noble foundation had been removed from its ancient premises near St Paul's Cathedral, in London, to the former estate of the poet Shelley's family near sleepy Horsham in Sussex. It was (and is) a magnificent, mighty school, but the scholars were by charter boys whose parents were poor, though not all of the same social degrees. In 1914 I had been at this school, which is known for such literary representatives as S.T. Coleridge and Charles Lamb and for all sorts of others in all walks of life, for six years and was on the staircase to the university. Lucky boys could look to Oxford or Cambridge in particular as they rose in classes in the school and could count on school exhibitions so long as at the finish they carried off university scholarships. Those would usually be concerned with classics or mathematics. They were worth about seventy or eighty pounds a year – amazing opulence! – or 'just enough'.

All at school went happily, occasionally hungrily, in most pastoral alluring surroundings and in an air well blending ancient and modern. There was a clear division between two tracks of education – classical and modern. A boy had to be placed, on his entering the school, in one of these two sides. My father firmly replied, 'Classical,' to the head-master's question on my first appearing, and probably that decision affected the unexpected experiences which were to follow. I missed, for instance, except for a few terms, the German classes, though French somehow was a stylish study abundantly available. That perhaps was due to an eager enthusiasm on the part of some masters for French literature and particularly French poetry. 'Modern' boys seemed rather to be involved in a commercial language.

Our acceptance of anything in classrooms can be imag-ined, and equally of our daily life altogether, well occupied from the early waking bell to the evening prayers called duty, and I must here note the description of our school, 'The religious, royal and ancient foundation of Christ's Hospital' – the temper of the place was distinctive. After nearly 400 years it could hardly be otherwise, even though we had been transplanted from town to country, wisely no doubt. The peace of the boys' lives would have been the same in the buildings of the old Greyfriars in London. These 'echoing cloisters pale', which are celebrated in a poem by Coleridge, remained, and they still do, as the calm pathway of the learned youths at the head of the school.

I have spoken of the peace which quite simply ruled our lives in our very orderly school, with its centuries of family spirit and useful duty continuing, and our Tudor uniform, the blue coats and yellow stockings, seeming to express a particular unity and concord among us; but there was one matter which did not harmonize, or so I used to feel in 1914. It looked to me as an influence directing the world, in its limited way, out of the paths of peace. All the boys – this was a recent ordinance – at quite an early age were required to become members of an officers training corps. This 'fine body of men' regularly paraded in accurate khaki uniform and often went afield for sham fights, charging over fields and up hillsides and letting off some noisy blank ammunition and generally trying to imagine what war itself would be like. From time to time these young warriors were paraded on the playing fields and inspected by a real general, who perhaps made a speech at the conclusion and might utter a view which I confess seemed to me a gloomy, even horrible view: We were not just playing soldiers; we should be 'wanted'. At school camp, in the holidays, with its diversions and realistic excitements, that note could be heard even without speeches. 'You'll be a man, my son.'

As the year 1914 wore on, the newspapers in the dayroom made us aware of troubles in Ireland which were regarded as capable of bringing on a fighting war, but for most of the busy little readers the political side of that crisis was too difficult. Presently, far away it was and seemed, a brutal assassination in some strange capital came into the news. To interpret its consequences was beyond us, but the occurrence was not be forgotten in a moment or two even while our beautiful peace and our almost untiring industry and great events like cricket cup ties and swimming sports went on. The summer holidays came into the prospect, and sunshine seemed likely to abound. Our military carbines would soon be stacked away in the armory, and our blue clothes, which made us rather conspicuous, except I suppose in London, could be exchanged for less antique and ornamental clothes at home.

We had our meals in the great dining-hall, and at the midday meal the housemasters would take their places at the top of the long tables. One day my own senior house-master came in, and as he sat down, with a curious ambiguous look, he said in a quiet way, 'Well boys, it looks as though within a month the whole of Europe will be at war.' This from him was something to be taken seriously, and it was. But I do not remember that any of us had any spoken comment to make. We were not prophets. In a way not all of us were surprised. But perhaps things would take another turn, and we had plenty on our hands – the immediate trouble was probably how to borrow a bicycle for the next enchanting Sunday afternoon ride though the rich byways of Sussex.

> Beat! beat! drums! – blow! bugles! blow!
> Through the windows – through doors – burst like a
> 　　　　　　　　　　　　　　　　ruthless force,
> Into the solemn church, and scatter the congregation,
> Into the school where the scholar is studying:
> Leave not the bridegroom quiet – no happiness must
> 　　　　　　　　　　　　he have now with his bride,
> Nor the peaceful farmer any peace, ploughing his field
> 　　　　　　　　　　　　　　or gathering his grain,
> So fierce you whirr and pound you drums – so shrill
> 　　　　　　　　　　　　　　　you bugles blow.

When World War I was declared, Walt Whitman's poems of 1861 did not obviously correspond to all that happened within my own observation in England in 1914, but they describe the effect of all as the new age established itself on our old world. When the diplomats gave up their riddle, and the world 'ultimatum' had become like the last trumpet or nearly, I was at home in our gentle village, and for a time – it would have been 'invasion country' if any were – there was excitement. My father even declared his intention of confronting any invaders as his front door, not the back door. The cleverest of all rumours was widely believed – the Russian Army, having dealt with Germany, would shortly be over the Channel and dealing with the United Kingdom. Meanwhile, some of our untalkative farm labourers and tradespeople quietly disappeared from

the scene, having 'jowned up' in one of the services or
another. And some young men who had come home from
business desks for summer holidays, masters of the great
world, suddenly looked quite as brilliant in well-fitting
uniforms.

Weeks were soon drifting by, and I could do much as
I liked, discovering other villages, catching carp, reading
and writing – and always listening to some wiseacre
announcing that the war would be over by Christmas. The
war somehow dodged our observation very annoyingly.
Summer holidays passed, and great victories went to sleep
again, and wearisome new songs drew attention to sewing
socks for soldiers or the long way to Tipperary. I was now
writing verses with great eagerness, but not often on the
war; what was near at hand usually started me off, and a
friendly bookseller in Shelley's old town was so kind as to
print a little volume or two for me, which at least kept me
from thinking too long about the prospect for those of my
age. The poems by the older generation in periodicals
which I came upon were mostly admonitions to us to join
the forces at once and be killed with all cheerfulness. The
penalties invented for not doing these things were severe:

> What will you lack, sonny, what will you lack
>   When the girls line up the street,
> Shouting their love to the lads come back
>   From the foe they rushed to beat?
> Will you send a strangled cheer to the sky
>   And grin till your cheeks are red?
> But what will you lack when your mates go by
>   With a girl who cuts you dead?

However, it was decided that the boys at our school who
were working for places in the universities should complete
their courses, which meant staying with one's books until
the summer of 1915. The girls whom I knew did not punish
me for that or present me with white feathers, as was a
reported fashion of those days.

On a glorious day that August I got out my bicycle for a longish ride across our county to Chichester, where the renowned Royal Sussex Regiment had its headquarters. I was equipped with papers which were to support my application for His Majesty's commission, and however dusty I was on arrival, the guard received me in the dignified way of an ancient regiment. A less bellicose place could hardly be imagined, and there seemed hardly any soldiers in it, but one was deputed to lead me to the major in charge of the barracks that day. He, too, put me at my ease at once, and I began to think the war was remarkably friendly after all. He told me to go over to the sergeant major and get him to run a tape measure round my chest and then come back for a drink and lunch. What promotion! The sequel perhaps a fortnight after was my receiving a commission and the outfit allowance – fifty pounds in that period was liberal. It easily covered the price – incidentally – of a sword.

Wearing this embarrassing romantic weapon, before many days I was travelling with other new subalterns to a training outfit at Weymouth, and still it was a pleasant war. We rose early for physical training on the beach, which exercise was broken off one morning by news that the British Army on the western front had made a successful attack at a place called Loos. It might be true; anyway it ended boredom, and following days gave the sceptics their opportunity. Altogether we were enjoying Weymouth without the holiday multitude when our orders arrived for doing something somewhere else, and I was one of those consigned to a large camp on the Sussex coast. We were so many that there were not enough 'other ranks' for us to play at officering, and the medical officer was exceedingly sympathetic in excusing us from duty, which let us disappear into joyous Brighton – or I would sometimes walk home, 20 miles, in those days.

Some of the second lieutenants in my hut had seen a bit of active service and had their curious experiences to tell, but not much about the small battles which I heard of as making life miserable on the western front. The idea of

everybody seemed to be to recite more outrageous limer-
icks and ballads than anybody else. Lectures and exercises
there were indeed, but it was argued that nothing in
training was in the least like the actual war, so why worry?
I was permitted without interference to collect around my
bed a library of books, some even of the eighteenth
century, the spoils of Brighton bystreets. These, however,
could not go with me on the next stage of this odd indolent
training – toward the end of 1915 the young officers found
themselves crossing a very angry midnight Irish Sea. The
destination was not many miles from Cork, a park with a
large ruined mansion and plenty of huts, a rifle range, and
very nice surrounding scenery.

Other arrangements had not been completed, and for
some days the most enterprising officers were searching the
country for supplies; I remember one of the plumpest of
them driving some pigs into camp; it was surprising how
soon the amateur organization for food and drink was
working. We were in this place, we gathered, partly because
of the state of Ireland and partly so as to be trained in
earnest by some powerful Guardsmen, one of whom was
soon nicknamed the Human Machine Gun. It came out
that we were to take at an early date an examination: to fail
would be, perhaps, not to be shot at dawn; to succeed
would mean to be sent promptly to that almost forgotten
place, the western front. So (and there were other reasons)
night schemes were better attended now than in the region
of Brighton, England.

In this camp, it is curious but pleasant to recall, I had
quite an allowance of talk about the English poets, ancient
and modern. The bed next to mine was occupied by one
of the descendants of Keats' friend Richards, a learned
reader indeed. Then one evening I was surprised and just
a shade frightened by a message from the adjutant, desiring
me to go see him. The reason was that he had heard something of my scribbling verses at the expense of some
prominent personalities in the camp, which he even
applauded, and soon we fell into serious discourse on

poetry. He could quote very choicely, and his taste then was for the sadder tones:

O to recall –
What to recall?

or 'Through the dark postern of time long elapsed…' I never saw Gordon Reah after this Irish episode, though once in the ramparts of Ypres in Belgium I had an affectionate note from him, and I did my utmost to get along the chaos and see him – but the attempt failed. It was an event, by the way, when I bought an edition of some of Tom Moore's Irish songs in Fermoy for one penny, 'as new.'

Early spring over southern Ireland and our songs as we ventured on the River Blackwater were disputing poetic rights in my mind when, having passed the threatened examination, I was with many friends on the way back to England, and once again the destination was that vast camp at Shoreham. This time I was given a daily job, marching a company of convalescent soldiers anywhere out of the way. They would not talk, though they were most amiable and humble, of their war. So I was still in the dark about it, more or less, when I found my name of the notice-board in the mess among those of subalterns who would 'proceed' to the British Expeditionary Force in two or three days. I should have been noisily glad, of course, but – some other time!

## II

The scene has changed indeed, and the month is May (1916). With two other young officers who have been on training with me, I am finding my way about in a quiet sector of the western front (but it has seen its bitter fighting) with one of our country battalions. A few miles east of these trenches (most of them are more or less passages between low embankments and sandbags) there is the big city of Lille, but except for hearing the city-hall clock strike midnight (or so we believe), it does not enter into our thoughts. Our landscape is flat, mostly, agricultural, and after nearly two years of war something of a wilderness. Here and there as we near the firing line we find a permanent-looking machine-gun emplacement built largely of brick, and the company headquarters look solid enough; but we also see a few ruins to suggest that artillery can swiftly obliterate such shelters.

The cheerfulness and attention to detail of those already experienced infantrymen with whom I now was have sounded on through my life as a simple music of an excellent old England. Even allusions to the Germans facing us over shattered fruit trees, deserted farm roads, hedges of crowded barbed wire, were quiet in tone and in thought. The ordinary references were to the Alleymans, Jerry, or Fritz. Even the two machine guns which were the greatest nuisance, as at night, from the German strongpoints had nicknames. As for firing, at that time and place the artillery took only a share now and then; but there was a strange and unforgettable performance from the rifles of both sides as day broke. Every man who had ammunition, on both sides, seemed to join in a great wave of shooting across no-man's-land, which swelled up and travelled along the line for ten minutes or a quarter of an hour and died down. This meant that about a mile behind the trenches the oddest noises of bullets swishing over or spinning from anything they hit surrounded us, walking from keep to dump, and the puzzle was, so far as we could observe, how seldom they caused casualties.

Danger there was in less obvious forms or methods. The firing lines twisted about so that often the enemy was able to look into a stretch of the other trenches, and from the snipers' posts a deadly shot might find its mark at any time. This uncertainty led to a superstitious quality in otherwise steady enough coming and going. The sun might glow long hours on a peaceful, even drowsy scene, but something was always lurking besides those frogs with their nightlong croaking and the more detested myriads of mosquitoes also claiming their ancient rights to the swampy pools. So, when it began to be remarked that the battalion was due to be relieved, and actually some officers and men had been named as an advance party to go back and arrange the company's billets, there was a slightly anxious thankfulness among us all, not simply owing to a need of rest. Nor was monotony quite the cause.

At that date, long-range firing was not much tried, and billets in small towns or villages were pleasant places, with the luxury of *estaminets* almost able to vie with the locals in England as scenes of mild refreshment and many anecdotes. But the war was not to be kept away even from rest areas, and often within a few hours of arrival in a more or less comfortable barn its requirement changed the outlook. Finding guards, for example, and drill and training almost caused revolutions, but no: much worse things could happen. There was 'something in the air'. Raids were perhaps being thought out, and indeed one of those operations on a grimly large scale was staged by the whole brigade with a great display of grenades, guns, trench mortars – and all to no purpose.

This attack was of the kind sometimes called Chinese attacks, or feints, and occurred on the day before the French and British armies began the Battle of the Somme, many miles south: its object was thought to have been the deceiving of the Germans into keeping some of their artillery away from that huge challenge, awaiting a new stroke in the north of the long line. Our battlefield adjoined the remains of the village Neuve-Chapelle, then famous as the objective of a greater assault a year and more earlier. But what was more conspicuous to our eyes, looking over the top of our breastwork front line for some days, was a gloomy wood, the Bois du Biez, with a few innocent-looking cottages along its hitherward edge, and in some way a legend emanated and circulated that this solid deep-green wood had been entered by British troops before in a 'censured' attack and not a man had come out of it.

Still, the new assault... A beautiful darkness ended, a sweet morning began, and there were some of us in a recognizable brewery ruin, waiting for the wonders. Right on the moment the flashes and thunders of our (then not too frightful) artillery began, and instantly from eastward quite an equivalent amazed us; where had been silence there seemed endless supplies of death, flame, and noise. We were saved at the moment in a small tunnel which the enemy himself had dug long ago. Then the slow day began; the poor chaps who were crossing no-man's-land and some of them carrying wooden bridges to defeat the deep drains dividing fields of rye or even tobacco, apart from 'the wire,' were stopped. Some hobbled and crawled home at last, as horrified by what they had seen happen to men (of whatever nation) as had almost happened to them. Their clothing and equipment told that part of the story. 'And I live.'

The June day grew quieter, and the sinister wood kept its secret. It seemed as though the Germans had forgotten the episode, but perhaps they had merely taken away the batteries that were to have been detained. Our front line had been, in spite of knocks, kept scrupulously neat, almost domesticated; now it was punched shapeless, scarcely passable, but in those days the farmlands which it traversed had their harmless look still, apart from some ancient deserted trenches with a reputation for horrors, mysteries.

All this may be termed in its context elementary education. So too other passages in that summer of siege warfare slightly revised. Hamlet commented some time earlier that:

> ... 'tis the sport to have the engineer
> Hoist with his own petard

and I believe he was alluding to the kind of war fought by the tunnellers with the co-operation of us footsoldiers, probably never again to achieve its vast, infernal perfections. Our chief observation of that kind of fighting came when we were sent into the line one side or another of the canal from Béthune to La Bassée (unprovocative little towns with Marlborough's wars of two centuries before haunting them quite without ghostly representatives in 1916). Here the landscape was fierce in a glaring sunlight, and industrial buildings in ruin hovered through the haze. When we took over a section of the parching front line, I talked with a philosophical engineer officer who remarked on the number of German mines known or suspected to be in construction underneath these trenches. And we, it was presumed, would have to occupy the place for a fortnight! In the end we emerged from that region and the one on the far side of the canal with mere examples of what might happen: we had had one small mine blown by the Germans underneath us, but a little short of a length, and had taken part in a loud bombing dispute following our own sappers' exploding a 'small mine' again, defensively, toward the enemy position. The first incident on a night streaming with rain and resounding and lanterning with scores of shellbursts was a bad one. 'It might have been worse,' but even Germans miscalculated. I remember that I had to make my way from our headquarters in a shaky brick cellar along glistening, soaked trenches I had never seen, and to find the real way after so many shells, until I was trying to say a word to a dying man, whose quiet manner by the dark canal bank was beyond any words then or now.

We grew, you may say cynically, accustomed to having things of this kind befall us, until we had seen many miles of the northward front line of the British Expeditionary Force and knew the unnatural history of numbers of death-dealing 'aerial torpedoes' – the word may serve for a whole genus of larger and smaller monsters – and evaded revolver shots in miraculous fashion. We had spells of emancipa-tion, and out of the trenches an officer had a right to an actual bedroom and a humpy but exquisitely clean bed in a cottage or perhaps a mansion. The summer of 1916 almost made it a throne. The real throne was perhaps the incomparable loving-kindness of all, officers and all, who lived and worked so much together, grumbling away at times, seeing past the war yet never judging their own fate. 'The British Army will all go home in one boat.' ... 'When this war ends, we shall see four blue lights go up.' 'No, mate, four black lights.' ... 'Here they come again, throwing gun and all at us.' ... 'They were shooting at our post with iron foundries.' ... 'Wind favourable for whizzbangs, Jim?' The last was a mild joke on the gas warnings, 'wind favourable' and the rest, which had become an ordinary part of the soldier's reading hereabouts.

To the next phase of our campaigning I shall not devote so much detail; the bewildering Battle of the Somme has been so often copiously described. We marched south toward it in golden weather and through what might have been described as France at peace. The roads were all cobblestone roads, and after our months in the mud of trenches the feet of many high-spirited soldiers were low-spirited; we passed the Guards marching equally, and indeed in the splendid heat and along those stone roads even they also seemed to be weary. We reached our attack area after an interval of rehearsals in a woodland and ploughland place west of Arras, said to be a facsimile of our assigned 'over the top'. If it was, it was no help in the frantic realities of the day when it came, then called Z day. The village which gave us a home during our exercises was perfect eighteenth century, a peasant picturesque dream in Corot's country. But soon, onward into a solitude; there the inhabitants had been withdrawn, and our position in a dusky wood was not only gas-scented but ghost-ridden – the sense of some intolerable presences had nothing to do with us, presumably, but that wood was deadly in gunfire fact and in some other way. Mailly Wood.

From here or near it the first of our three main ordeals in the Somme battles was begun. Begun, but the misery of being ordered up to the line and sent back for postpone-ment was repeated a time or two. The first actual attack on a glowing autumn day – it opened before daylight and hardly a man had any chance of knowing the ups and downs of the hollow to be crossed on the way to the

enemy's line – was an obliteration. It was completely mysterious: the troops just disappeared. Perhaps the Germans'
deep dugouts, especially those under the railway embank-
ment on our right, were too many for the bombers
especially. No message came from those merry boys, no
acknowledgment of new supplies of hand grenades.
Further, as we were on the little hills sloping toward the
Ancre River's north side, the German guns on the hills
opposite, their destruction of the unlucky British infantry
attacking there having been easy for them, had no trouble
in switching to us, and the network camouflage over our
little slit trenches soon vanished, and our headquarters
were simple targets.

So we were 'a complete failure', and there were miles of
that; but southward the armies made some progress over
the most terrifying devastated area perhaps ever yet seen on
our planet. I remember coming in sight of it for the first
time: gunnery had extinguished every sign of life every step
to the horizon and left a specimen of a world without a
God. But the battle went on. We were used as a holding
battalion, securing miles of front, as the autumn also went
on. Late in October our function changed, and we again
attacked. 'We' now meant almost a new battalion, so many
reinforcements had been called for, poor fellows, many of
who made their short acquaintance with modern war in
the moment of mad battle itself. They largely fell in the
next two days. The battle took place in white frost and
began in full daylight. Underfoot was mud or corpses. We
somehow gained Stuff Trench, and such was its desolation
that the battalion relieving us (they had to be led in almost
individually) hated it and us, too (a rare thing).

November brought clammy fogs and deeper mud,
besides war itself, and a third attack was required of us. It
was successful! The Germans were betrayed by their enormous deep dugouts. But nothing much came of that. The
*Sommeschlacht* (Battle of the Somme) was somehow wearing
out. It had introduced the tanks to the fighting man's world.
We saw some examples, heard of their wonders, and

dragged ourselves along. Then one night our grand colonel for once spoke out and said that we were to be taken out of the Somme battle, immediately. And we were – those who then made up 'we' – and again were men marching, with even our band playing us into unspoiled Doullens (the stretcher-bearers formed the band). Where were we going?

North this time, to a city with a glory about it but also an air of mortality – Ypres in Belgium. Of course, in incurable ruins, but serviceable as the stronghold of the Ypres Salient, a pattern of trenches of all sorts defying any advance of the German powers that way to the Channel ports. It had been tolerably quiet during 1916 but was constantly under observation and frequently under heavy fire. It was managed by the British garrison in a businesslike way, thanks especially to the ancient ramparts which guarded the grey, lifeless city on the east side. They are still standing over the lovely moat, which even in war was beautiful with swans. They conceal many spacious excavations, usually safe protections, in our time – at any time since perhaps the Romans held outposts here.

But we had no leisure or inspiration to think of other legions in Flanders. A dismal and painful winter was seizing the Ypres Salient when we rather amazedly arrived. Going out of the place to the area of Hill 60 on reconnaissance, my dear Sergeant Wally Ashford, walking with me through a grove of skeleton trees, remarked, with his ambiguous grin, 'Looks just like the Somme… well, rather worse.' It bore the strange title Sanctuary Wood. It had been no sanctuary to generations of doomed young soldiers of several nationalities.

Intense winter ended the year 1916 in those parts and went on without mercy until sudden kind spring poured sunshine over the snow and ice. Fighting and digging had gone on, but now that mercy seemed to descend, it was apparent that the year 1917 was to produce war of a new ferocity and, as many ordinary soldiers thought, futility. The name Passchendaele is inscribed on that page of war history. It was intended at first that, from Ypres, the low ridge of Passchendaele and other uninteresting farmland round it should be captured in the spring. The ridge was said to overlook the English Channel, and if it did, it could not worry the British Navy. But it had a good view, and so did other low uplands, of everything in or around muti-lated Ypres. A further intention of the battle was to advance as far as Ostend.

'That agony returns.' On July 31 the worst and most hated of the British offensives was begun, against all reason, all around or nearly all around Ypres. Reason had had no luck for weeks before; the preparations, including new roads and railways everywhere into the forward area, had been fantastically shown off, as though the Germans would be scared by the exhibition. The farmlands over which we were to advance had been drained in former times with minute care, and now that honest, wise labour was all lost with the increasing bombardments – and the weather. It was well known that at the end of July Flanders weather almost inevitably became foul.

On July 31 then, as the darkness was dying, the Pass-chendaele battle began with an orgy of gunfire and of machine-gun barrages which I thought noisier than all the artillery, and on our share of the line we were surprised to get across entanglements and tattered trenches without extraordinary difficulty. We soon found the concrete block-houses which the Germans had been building for their defence system, often within barns and farmhouses, great and small, but the principle of the opening of the defence was mainly to withdraw the majority of the troops. As any rate we moved forward and, when we had reached the posi-tions to be seized were even bewildered by having done so – at a price. But we for a moment felt that success had beamed on us. The other side's guns were not doing much just then. Another enemy came into action. Almost silently the rain began. It went on, grew heavier, and the vision of victory dissolved in the greyness.

To try and chronicle the miseries and destructions of the days thus begun would be to invite sleepless nights or insane dreams, which have been exorcised, in any event, during the half century, and the battle with its variations of place and problem had my attention until summer had become winter, and however I was released from it (the authorities had not been altogether monsters, but had laid on a scheme of schools behind the line which were perhaps rest stations, as well as places of instruction), I was still back among the captured concrete pillboxes. The natural history of these was that their entrances, once we had possession, faced the German guns, and so always a direct hit from them was especially murderous. It was so on the celebrated Menin Road, in royal autumn sunshine, at the end of September 1917. We could not avoid these concrete shelters, but the German gunners had them before them whenever they cared to bump them. Sunshine and irony united then. But late in the year a brilliant surprise far to the south, a tank battle toward Cambrai, diverted the war proper for a few days. 'Think we shall win?' It was almost a possibility.

What ideas were now going around among the fighting men? Not many more than usual, but that America's armies were in the business was knowingly mentioned by some not loquacious sergeants. Our performances became a little less urgent, I thought, though hardly less deathly. At the end of that year of pain, 1917, it was strange for me to be in freezing starshine, staring east over the death-strewn miles, waiting for the rival guns to say something. They did, but as though bored. 'How long, O Lord, how long?'

Before long we had moved far south to the Cambrai battlefield and been happy to find comparatively dry green ground and firm roads around our front line. The remains of the recent contest, which was a wonderful performance on both sides, offered no early end to the war. My expectation of being on the scene, God willing, through the new year, 1918, was simple; old friends were still there; the comforts were tolerable, and it was said we should soon have leave to visit Amiens even. But a system of transferring some who had a certain front-line length of experience had begun, and it included me. It happened so while we were digging miles of trenches and putting out entanglements of barbed wire apparently against a German offensive of considerable depth. It was assigned to me to prepare defence orders for our front. That done, and even approved by our commanding officer, I was – away!

The hope of returning to the line may seem to have been a symptom of madness, but such a hope stirred in me in a camp in England, and I nearly got back, when the German attack anticipated had roared itself along far beyond our trace trenches. The half-starved German soldiery and civilians could not now quite win, and my next contribution to the declining battle was in November, 1918, when the war was slackening from several causes into its mortification. A godforsaken winter followed the Armistice, but at any rate the guns were silent; the starvation state of affairs went on but could not go on forever; the last booby trap of the German retreat had at length compelled amazement if it had failed to kill.

What out of all this miscellany abides, after so long? The war cemeteries. But somebody was saying lately, when viewing one of them with 20,000 graves in it (near Passchendaele), such a total was only chick feed in comparison with other displays of inhumanity. Then, perhaps what goes on is the memory of anonymous heroes, who personally had nothing to hope for and who had nothing 'patriotic' to say and went on day after day with a countenance of invincibility, not notably referring to any known enemy, just facing whatever gods may be.

Published in *Promise of Greatness – The War of 1914–1918*, edited by George A. Panichas (New York, 1968), to commemorate the 50th anniversary of the Armistice.

# NOTES

## Sources

Edmund Blunden, *Undertones of War*, with an introduction by Hew
 Strachan (London: Penguin Modern Classics, 2010)
Martin Chown, *A Companion Guide to Edmund Blunden's* Undertones of
 War (The Edmund Blunden Society, 2011)
B.J. Kirkpatrick, *A Bibliography of Edmund Blunden* (Oxford: Oxford
 University Press, 1979)
Helen McPhail and Phillip Guest, *On the Trail of the Poets of the Great War
 – Edmund Blunden* (Barnsley: Leo Cooper, 1999)
Barry Webb, *Edmund Blunden – A Biography* (New Haven and London:
 Yale University Press, 1990)
The Wakefield Family History Sharing site is very useful for its slang
 dictionary: http://www.wakefieldfhs.org.uk

## Introduction

1 Blunden, letter to Siegfried Sassoon, 21 June 1930, quoted by Webb,
 *Edmund Blunden*, p. 98.
2 'Old Homes', *Poems of Many Years* (1957).
3 One of his students was the poet Keith Douglas, who was killed in
 the Normandy landings of 1944; they kept up a regular correspondence during the war, and Blunden sent his poems on to T.S. Eliot at
 Faber. Their temperaments were very different, but their mutual
 respect arose, no doubt, from the shared experience of combat, as
 well as from Blunden's affinity with an alumnus of Christ's Hospital.
 See Keith Douglas, *The Letters*, edited by Desmond Graham
 (Manchester, 2000).
4 See Webb, *Edmund Blunden*, p. 205.
5 Blunden, letter to Claire Poynting, quoted by Webb, *Edmund Blunden*,
 pp. 233–34.
6 Randall Stevenson, *Literature and the Great War 1914–1918* (Oxford,
 2013), has an interesting section on the importance of song to the
 troops, 'In music halls and theatres, in concert parties – or played on
 the "eternal gramophone" Max Plowman recalls hearing everywhere, even in the trenches', p. 123.
7 Quoted by Webb, *Edmund Blunden*, p. 101.

8   'Reunion in War', *The Shepherd and Other Poems of Peace and War* (1922).

9   Quoted by Webb, *Edmund Blunden*, pp. 170–71.

10 Jon Stallworthy, *Anthem for Doomed Youth: Twelve Soldier Poets of the First World War* (London, 2002), p. 179.

11 'The handsomely bound book issued by G.A. Blunden delights my eye. It is a *real* book. (I haven't read it yet.)' This is followed by a letter of 4 November in which Sassoon admits, 'I haven't so much as snipped the pages yet, as I am reading a type-written work by T.E. Shaw' (it was T.E. Lawrence's *The Mint*). In the published correspondence, Blunden does not press him for an opinion – perhaps they simply talked about it. *Selected Letters of Siegfried Sassoon and Edmund Blunden*, edited by Carol Z. Rothkopf (London, 2012), vol. I, pp. 298, 301.

12 Paul Fussell, *The Great War and Modern Memory* (Oxford, 1975), p. 268.

13 Quoted by Stevenson, *Literature and the Great War*, pp. 48–49. MacDiarmid (Christopher Grieve) joined up in 1915, served in the RAMC in Salonika, Greece and France, and was invalided out in 1918.

14 Blunden uses a phrase from Sir Thomas Browne's *Urne-Burial* (1658), the opening of Chapter V: 'Now since these dead bones have already outlasted the living ones of *Methuselah*, and in a yard under ground, and thin walls of clay, out-worn all the strong and specious buildings above it; and quietly rested under the drums and tramplings of three conquests: what Prince can promise such diuturnity unto his Reliques, or might not gladly say, *Sic ego componi versus in ossa velim*. Time, which antiquates Antiquities, and hath an art to make dust of all things, hath yet spared these *minor* monuments.'

15 Ford joined up in 1915, aged 42, worked in the military transport section, and was posted back to Britain in 1917. This comment is reported by Wyndham Lewis, and quoted by Stevenson, *Literature and the Great War*, p. 87. Ford went on to write the best of the war novels, his *Parade's End* tetralogy, the first of which was published in 1924, ahead of the mass of war writing that started to appear at the end of the 1920s.

16 Jon Stallworthy, in his Introduction to the Folio Society edition of *Undertones of War*, which includes *De Bello Germanico* (London, 1989), p. xi. He continues: 'The earlier version is more documentary, contains a higher proportion of direct speech, but at the same time is less dramatic', and concludes (p. xii), 'The difference is almost that between prose and poetry. G.S. Fraser, indeed, once called *Undertones* "the best war poem".'

17 Stevenson, *Literature and the Great War*, p. 64.

18 Ford, 'A Day of Battle', quoted by Alan Judd, *Ford Madox Ford* (London, revised edition 1991), pp. 288–89.

19 Sarah Cole, *Modernism, Male Friendship, and the First World War*

(Cambridge, 2003), p. 140. Liddell Hart had the rank of Captain when he fought at the Somme, and was sent home to train soldiers after being badly gassed.

20 Robert Graves, *Goodbye to All That* (London, 1929; Harmondsworth, 1960), p. 157.

21 Cole, *Modernism*, p. 149.

22 Cole, *Modernism*, p. 158. Joseph Lee (1876–1949) was a Scottish poet, artist and journalist who joined up in 1914 and became a prisoner of war in 1917.

23 Webb, *Edmund Blunden*, p. 70.

24 Webb, *Edmund Blunden*, p. 94.

25 Blunden conveys their humour and inventiveness but not their swearing, constrained like other writers by publishing conventions, and perhaps by his own temperament. Private David Jones writes in his Preface that 'the whole shape of our discourse was conditioned by such words [...] The very repetition of them made them seem liturgical, certainly deprived them of malice, and occasionally [...] gave a kind of significance, and even at moments a dignity, to our speech. Sometimes their juxtaposition in a sentence, and when expressed under poignant circumstances, reached real poetry.' *In Parenthesis* (London, 1937; 1963), p. xii.

26 Quoted by Webb, *Edmund Blunden*, p. 44.

27 Quoted by David Reynolds, *The Long Shadow: The Great War and the Twentieth Century* (London, 2013), p. 344, who agrees that Blunden 'left an indelible mark on our understanding of what constitutes "war poetry"'.

28 Paul Fussell reflects on the difference between 'modern' and 'modernist' writers and their attitudes in his essay 'Modernism, Adversary Culture and Edmund Blunden', in *Killing in Verse and Prose and Other Essays* (London, 1988), pp. 245–70.

## De Bello Germanico

*De Bello Gallico*
Properly *Commentarii de bello Gallico*, a memoir by Julius Caesar of his campaigns in Gaul from 58 to 52 BC.

D—
Blunden's companion is named in *Undertones* as [G.W.] Doogan, 'a plump, ironical, unscareable Irishman' (p. 6). Second Lieutenant Doogan was killed by a shell after the capture of Stuff Trench in October 1916, and his name is on the Thiepval Memorial (McPhail and Guest, *On the Trail of the Poets*, p. 76).

RE
A Royal Engineer: commonly known as 'sappers', the REs provided technical and engineering support to the army.

Ph. Gibbs
Probably a reference to Philip Gibbs (1877–1962), one of five official British war reporters during the First World War. He wrote for the *Daily Telegraph* and *Daily Chronicle*, and published a series of books: *The Soul of the War* (1915), *The Battle of the Somme* (1917), *From Bapaume to Passchendaele* (1918) and *The Realities of War* (1920).

estaminet
A village pub/café in France serving basic food, alcohol and coffee.

E.A. Poe's Auber
Edgar Allan Poe's poem 'Ulalume' (1847) begins in October, 'hard by the dim lake of Auber, / In the misty mid region of Weir…'. The Battle of Aubers Ridge took place in May 1915.

whizzbang
A light shell fired from a field gun.

'British Warm'
The double-breasted overcoat of khaki wool issued to soldiers or bought by officers – for an illustration, see http://www.paoyeomanry.co.uk/LYUnifromWW1.htm (accessed 3 January 2014).

bullets or five-nines
Blunden refers to the 5.9 inch German artillery shell, also mentioned by Wilfred Owen in 'Dulce et Decorum Est'.

Jocks
Soldiers from Scottish regiments.

Colonel
Lieutenant Colonel H.J. Grisewood was the commander of the 11th Royal Sussex, described by Blunden as 'very grave and conscientious' (*Undertones*, p. 10). He relinquished his command in June 1916 after resisting an order to attack a heavily fortified section of the German line (see Hew Strachan, introduction to *Undertones*, p. x). His brother, Francis Grisewood, was killed a week later 'in another abortive attack' (McPhail and Guest, *On the Trail of the Poets*, p. 35).

Company Commander
Captain Penruddock[e], two years older than Blunden, was killed in

action on the Somme in September 1916 (McPhail and Guest, *On the Trail of the Poets*, p. 67): 'as I see him in the pool of time gone by, he appears as a boy, fair-haired, fine-eyed and independent of experience' (*Undertones*, p. 18).

the Fat Boy
Joe, the boy who eats great quantities of food and is always falling asleep in *The Posthumous Papers of the Pickwick Club* by Charles Dickens (1837).

Maconachie
Tinned vegetable stew, named after the manufacturer.

'fell to with an appetite'
The last words that Charles Dickens wrote, in his unfinished novel *Edwin Drood* (1870).

Archibalds
Anti-aircraft guns, also known as 'Archies'.

Pushful Percies
*The Magnet*, a boys' weekly paper, was created in the years before the war by Percy Griffiths, whose nickname was 'Pushful Percy'; perhaps a general reference to those who were keen to push the line forward; the battle of the Somme was supposed to be the Allies' 'Big Push'.

Baby Elephants
The Wakefield Family History website (http://www.wakefieldfhs.org.uk) defines an 'elephant' as a small dugout reinforced with semi-circular sheets of corrugated iron; presumably this is a variant name.

Pipsqueak
A small-calibre shell or a rifle grenade.

Minnie
Abbreviation of the German *Minenwerfer*, 'mine thrower', a form of trench mortar.

Ack emma
Morning: a.m.

L—
Second Lieutenant Richard Limbery-Buse, with whom Blunden was 'as thick as thieves', survived wounds and shell-shock, left the army in 1919 and later emigrated to California (McPhail and Guest, *On the Trail of the Poets*, pp. 33–34).

rum-jars
In this context mortar bombs, similar in shape to the earthenware jars in which the rum ration was issued to troops.

Very lights
These were fired from a pistol and used to shine a light on no-man's-land and also to signal; named after Samuel W. Very.

cap comforters
A knitted woollen cylinder that could be pulled over the head 'as a warm alternative to the service dress cap'; for information and an illustration, see http://www.iwm.org.uk/collections/item/object/30101240 (accessed 4 January 2014).

Shelleian shakedown of roses
P.B. Shelley, 'Music, when soft voices die' (written 1821): 'Roseleaves, when the rose is dead, / Are heaped for the beloved's bed…'.

great and murderous battle here a year ago
This refers to the second Battle of Ypres, 22 April–25 May 1915, in which the BEF casualties were triple those of the Germans.

BEF
British Expeditionary Force – the force that was dispatched to France in 1914 and remained for the duration.

bully beef
Tinned corned beef, eaten hot or cold.

duff
A flour pudding, boiled in a bag or steamed.

The General
Brigadier-General M.L. Hornby, whose behaviour Blunden describes in *Undertones*, summing him up as 'this singular man, whom we all found difficult, and whom we honour'(p. 16).

ASC
Army Service Corps, which conveyed supplies of all kind – food, equipment, ammunition – to the front lines.

Gilbert White
White (1720–93) was a curate in his home village of Selborne, Hampshire, and his correspondence with two distinguished naturalists was the basis for his popular *Natural History and Antiquities of Selborne* (1788).

drowsed with the fume of poppies
John Keats, 'Ode to Autumn' (1820): 'Drows'd with the fume of poppies, while thy hook / Spares the next swath and all its twined flowers…'.

native woodnotes
John Milton, 'L'Allegro' (1645): 'Or sweetest Shakespeare, Fancy's child / Warble his native wood-notes wild…'.

'thoro' mud, thoro' wire'
Blunden is playing on the fairy's reply to Puck: 'Over hill, over dale, / Thorough bush, thorough brier, / Over park, over pale, / Thorough flood, thorough fire'; William Shakespeare, *A Midsummer Night's Dream*, II.1.

mute and inglorious
Thomas Gray, 'Elegy Written in a Country Churchyard' (1751): 'Some mute inglorious Milton here may rest…'

'An enemy hath done this'
Matthew 13:28: 'He said unto them, An enemy hath done this. The servants said unto him, Wilt thou then that we go and gather them up?'

Batman
He is mentioned several times in *Undertones* as [W.E.] Shearing, last seen 'wearing his Military Medal for admirable courage in last September's Menin Road massacre' (p. 189).

I snatched a fearful joy
Thomas Gray, 'Ode on a Distant Prospect of Eton College' (1747): 'Still as they run they look behind, / They hear a voice in every wind, / And snatch a fearful joy.'

Johnson Hole
The impact of a German 15 cm artillery shell; named after Jack Johnson, the world-famous first African-American heavyweight boxing champion (1908–15). Some derivations suggest this was because of the black smoke, some that the shell itself was black, but clearly it was also a tribute to the power of the shell.

K—
Edmond Xavier Kapp (1890–1978), artist, who joined the Press Bureau in June 1916, becoming 'a temporary proprietor of motor-cars and châteaux' (*Undertones*, p. 163).

'Great Tom is cast'
This is a traditional round, on the subject of the bells of Christ Church
Cathedral, Oxford.


Vimy
Vimy Ridge, north-east of Arras, provided a clear and long view of the
surrounding territory, and was taken by the Germans in October 1914.
The French tried to re-take it twice in 1915, then the British took over
their positions in 1916 and discovered that the Germans had built an
extensive network of tunnels and mines in the area. On 21 May the
Germans attacked the British lines, with furious shelling, and succeeded
in capturing about a thousand yards of trenches. Counter-attacks were
unsuccessful. British wounded, killed and missing amounted to about
2,500. 'The hardest hit battalion was the 1/8 London (Post Office Rifles)
which alone lost over 90 men, killed in the initial bombardment.' (See
http://www.cwgc.org/media/35163/general_sir_henry_wilson_and_
the_disaster_at_vimy.pdf, accessed 4 January 2014). The Canadian
Corps finally took the Ridge during the Battle of Arras, 1917.


like the deaf adder…
Psalm 58: 4-5: 'Their poison is like the poison of a serpent: they are like
the deaf adder that stoppeth her ear; / Which will not harken to the
voice of charmers, charming never so wisely.'


'a tale, a dream'
John Masefield, *Lollingdon Downs*, VIII (1917):

> The Kings go by with jewelled crowns
> Their horses gleam, their banners shake, their spears are many.
> The sack of many-peopled towns
> Is all their dream:
> The way they take
> Leaves but a ruin in the break,
> And, in the furrow that the ploughmen make,
> A stampless penny, a tale, a dream.

Masefield (1878–1967) had been rejected for war service when he volun-
teered, aged 36, but he served in France as a British Red Cross orderly
in 1915, and at Gallipoli working in the ambulance service. He went
back to France 1916–17, and was commissioned to write a book on the
Somme campaign. He became Poet Laureate in 1930. Webb describes
his relationship with Blunden as 'always cordial though never close'
(*Edmund Blunden*, p. 112).


'to face the naked days'
Rudyard Kipling's poem 'All we have and are' (1914) includes the lines:

Comfort, content, delight,
The ages' slow-bought gain,
They shrivelled in a night.
Only ourselves remain
To face the naked days
In silent fortitude,
Through perils and dismays,
Renewed and re-renewed.

Oilcan, the Pineapple and the Woolly Bear
A trench mortar bomb; a Mills bomb; German shrapnel explosion.

Honni soit!
*Honi soit qui mal y pense*, 'Shame on him who thinks ill of it', is the motto on the Order of the Garter and is also incorporated in the badges of several British and Commonwealth regiments, including the Royal Engineers.

'deliberate instancy'
Francis Thompson (1859–1907), 'The Hound of Heaven': 'But with unhurrying chase, / And unperturbed pace, / Deliberate speed, majestic instancy, / They beat – '.

Walton
Izaak Walton (1593–1683), author of *The Compleat Angler* (1653, 1655), a mixture of dialogues, prose and verse on the subject of fishing. Blunden wrote that his taste for book collecting was formed in childhood by little books with rich decorations on the covers: 'Walton was festooned with golden creels and rods and lines and trout and bulrushes; the old man himself [...] stood for ever there by the hawthorn bush, baiting his hook, about to throw in again'; 'Bringing them Home', in *The Mind's Eye* (London, 1934), p. 233.

a new Company Commander
Neville [Bulwer-]Lytton (1879–1951), artist and journalist. He was the son of Robert Bulwer-Lytton, first Earl of Lytton and Viceroy of India, who published several volumes of poetry under the name Owen Meredith. Neville Lytton finished his book *The Press and the General Staff* (1920) with the words: 'I came to the conclusion that no one but a madman could ever wish for war; the highly polished boots, the bright buttons, the glittering medals and the clicking of spurred heels must never again deceive humanity into thinking that war is anything but the blackest tragedy from start to finish.' See http://ww1centenary.oucs.ox.ac.uk/material/the-art-of-remembering-the-neville-lytton-first-world-war-frescos-and-the-balcombe-victory-hall (accessed 4 January 2014).

Little Tich
Harry Relph (1867–1928) was a famous English music-hall comedian and dancer, four feet six inches tall.

O. Henry
The pen-name of the popular American writer William Sydney Porter (1862–1910), known for his short stories with their twist or surprise at the end.

'on indent'
On order. The *Wipers Times* described a quartermaster as 'a bird of strange habits:– when attacked covers itself with indents and talks backwards'. (Quoted by Stevenson in *Literature and the Great War*, p. 18.)

Jutland
This naval battle between Britain and Germany was fought on 31 May–1 June 1916 in the North Sea near Jutland, Denmark. Fourteen British and eleven German ships were sunk; both sides claimed victory and it remains a debated battle.

Horatio
A reference to the character in Shakespeare's *Hamlet*, perhaps; he first appears with other soldiers on the watch and sees Hamlet's father's ghost.

C—
Second Lieutenant A.E. Charlwood, 'inclined to stammer, who as I soon found out had played cricket for Sussex' (*Undertones*, p.11); he later joined the Royal Flying Corps.

Feel his bumps
This refers to phrenology, the idea that the physical shape of a person's head indicates mental qualities. Blunden could be referring to a dinner Charles Lamb attended on 28 December 1817, recounted by the painter and diarist Benjamin Robert Haydon: 'After an awful pause, the comptroller [of stamps] said, "Don't you think Newton a great genius?" I could not stand it any longer. Keats put his head into my books. Ritchie squeezed in a laugh. Wordsworth seemed asking himself "Who is this?" Lamb got up, and taking a candle, said, "Sir, will you allow me to look at your phrenological development?" He then turned his back on the poor man […] It was indeed an immortal evening.' E.V. Lucas, *The Life of Charles Lamb* (London, 1905), I, pp. 393–94.

Stokes, Newton Pippins
Varieties of apple.

picric
An acid used in explosives.

Neuve Chapelle
The battle here 10–13 March 1915 enabled the British to break through German lines, but the advantage could not be sustained. Of the 40,000 Allied troops taking part, there were 7,000 British and 4,200 Indian casualties.

## War and Peace

'sweeps with all its lessening towers'
Alfred, Lord Tennyson, 'In Memoriam', XI: 'Calm and still light on yon great plain / That sweeps with all its autumn bowers, / And crowded farms and lessening towers'. Blunden was reading Tennyson at the Front in 1917, and notes in a letter: 'But literature languishes as a whole in the battalion except for two books (*Flossie* and *Aphrodite*) which the Arch-bishop of Canterbury has probably not read.' Quoted by Webb, *Edmund Blunden*, p. 73.

Mr Hardy's *Dynasts*
Thomas Hardy, *The Dynasts* (1906–1908), a three-part epic verse drama of the Napoleonic wars, described by George Orwell in an article for the *Tribune* (18 September 1942) as 'a grandiose and rather evil vision of armies marching and counter-marching through the mists, and men dying by hundreds of thousands in the Russian snows, and all for absolutely nothing'. Blunden knew and admired Hardy, and published a biography of the novelist and poet, *Thomas Hardy* (1942). On his death in 1926, as a memento of Blunden's visits to Max Gate, Mrs Hardy presented him with Hardy's copy of Edward Thomas's *Poems* (Webb, *Edmund Blunden*, p. 135).

## Aftertones

the camp
This was the training camp at Stowlangtoft, in Suffolk.

court of inquiry ... romance
Blunden had to give evidence; he afterwards went for a drink in Newmarket with fellow officers, and was served by a local girl, Mary Daines. As the inquiry progressed, Blunden made the most of the opportunities of seeing her, and on 1 June 1918 they were married: he was twenty-one and she was eighteen.

'out of all this great big world they'd chosen me'
Adapted from the popular Jerome Kern lyric, 'They Didn't Believe Me'
(from the musical *The Girl from Utah*, 1914): 'They'll never believe me /
That from this great big world / You've chosen me'.

'Water, water, everywhere'
Samuel Taylor Coleridge, *The Rime of the Ancient Mariner*, II, 119.

G.H. Harrison
Colonel George Hyde Harrison (1877–1964), commander of the 11th
Royal Sussex at Festubert, the Somme and in the early days of Ypres, of
whom Blunden wrote in *Undertones*, 'his likeness cannot come again in
this life, nor can man be more beloved' (p. 110).

*Life of Keats*
Blunden recounts that he found a copy of Edward Thomas's *Keats* (1916)
in a hole in the wall beside his bed when billeted in Arras. Thomas had
died in April 1917, at the beginning of the Battle of Arras, and Blunden
hoped that this might have been the poet's own copy of the book: 'I
fancied that I could see the tall, Shelley-like figure of the poet gathering
together his equipment for the last time, hastening out of this ruined
building to join his men and march into battle, and forgetting his copy
of John Keats.' (Quoted from an unpublished reminiscence, Webb,
*Edmund Blunden*, p. 56.)

Wolseyan youth
A reference to Cardinal Wolsey (1473–1530), whose portrait in Christ
Church, Oxford, shows a man of large girth.

I read Elia
*The Essays of Elia* (1823) by Charles Lamb (1775–1834) includes an essay
on Christ's Hospital, the school Lamb attended, and of which Blunden
was very proud to be a pupil. Blunden chose Lamb as the subject of his
Clark Lectures at Cambridge in 1932. A discerning book collector,
Blunden believed that he had Lamb's own copy of Milton.

Bouchain
The town was held by the French and besieged for 34 days by the Duke
of Marlborough in his last campaign, in 1711. Eugene of Savoy was
Marlborough's partner in some famous military victories, but had gone
to the Rhine at this point in the War of the Spanish Succession.

the new influenza
It is estimated that this virulent strain of influenza killed from 50 to 100
million people worldwide in 1918–19, particularly affecting young

adults. Reports of the pandemic were muted in post-war Europe but uncensored in neutral Spain, thus it became known as 'Spanish flu'.

## The Somme Still Flows

'the lucky lads'
Blunden's poem 'Zero' was titled 'Come on, my lucky lads' when printed in *Undertones of War*. Eric Partridge, in his *Dictionary of Catchphrases* (1977, 1985), notes that this phrase – with the variant 'Come on, you don't want to live forever!' – was addressed by sergeant-majors to the troops as a rallying cry before they scrambled out of the trenches. It may have dated back to the Napoleonic wars.

'We're going South'
This sentence haunted Blunden, as the prelude to the march to the Somme; it appears in his poem 'Two Voices' (1924), included in *Undertones*.

## We Went to Ypres

Vauban
The Marquis de Vauban (1633–1707), the foremost military engineer of the period, was famous for designing fortifications, including the Ramparts at Ypres, next to the Menin Gate.

the new Menin Gate
This was the first of the Imperial (now Commonwealth) War Graves Commission's Memorials to the Missing, and contains names on stone panels of nearly 55,000 Commonwealth soldiers who died in the Ypres Salient but whose bodies have never been identified or found. Designed by Reginald Blomfield and opened on 24 July 1927, it was condemned by Blunden's friend Siegfried Sassoon in his poem 'On Passing the New Menin Gate', which speaks of 'those doomed, conscripted unvictorious ones … the intolerably nameless names'.

my friend C.
W.J. Collyer, an 'Old Blue' (Christ's Hospital pupil), killed in action at St Julien, 31 July 1917.

'windy corner'
'windy' was trench slang for being afraid; north-west of the village of Cuinchy there is a Guards cemetery at Windy Corner.

**The Extra Turn**

'King's Horses, and Men'
This was a fox-trot lyric by Noel Gay and Harry Graham that was a hit
in London in 1930–31; the music was used as the opening theme for
Laurel and Hardy's *The Music Box* (1932) (http://www.laurel-and-hardy.
com/films/talkies/music-music.html, accessed 30 December 2013).

Mr George Robey
George Robey (1869–1954), English music-hall star, probably best
known for singing 'If You Were the Only Girl in the World'. *The Bing
Boys Are Here: A Picture of London Life in a Prologue and Six Panels* was a series
of revues that ran at the Alhambra Theatre in London, beginning in
April 1916 with Robey in the cast.

'Another little drink wouldn't do us any harm'
A song by Clifford Grey (1887–1941), written in 1916, the same year as
his famous 'If You Were the Only Girl in the World'. Herbert Asquith
was the Liberal Prime Minister from 1908 to 1916, when he resigned,
and was not a successful wartime leader.

Flying Pigs
Bombs fired by a trench mortar.

Sidneian virtue
A reference to Sir Philip Sidney (1554–86), who died of wounds received
in battle in the Netherlands, and was considered to be a perfect Renais-
sance man: poet, patron, soldier, lover, courtier.

as in Milton's vision
John Milton, *Paradise Lost*, IV, 598–99: 'Now came still ev'ning on, and
twilight gray / Had in her sober livery all things clad'.

Pratt
Noted In *Undertones* for 'charmingly' parrying the Colonel's suggestions,
but 'killed soon afterwards' (p. 80); possibly Archibald Pratt, killed in
action June 1916.

Brock's benefit
A spectacular display of pyrotechnics, from the name of the public fire-
works display held annually at the Crystal Palace, London, from 1865 to
1936, from C.T. Brock, firework manufacturer (Elizabeth Knowles,
'Brock's benefit', *The Oxford Dictionary of Phrase and Fable*, 2006; *Encyclo-
pedia.com* accessed 30 December 2013).

Lintott
'Jake' Lintott, 'the clever assistant adjutant who had been with the Canadians at Ypres' (*Undertones*, p. 62), last mentioned as 'having collapsed and disappeared in a deathly state from among us' (p. 132).

Millward
Major William Colsey Millward was to succeed Harrison in charge of the battalion. Apparently he was one of the very few privates to rise up through the ranks and attain that of (Acting) Brigadier during the First World War; he won the DSO and the Croix de Guerre, and lost a leg in October 1918.

'even in the cannon's mouth'
William Shakespeare, *As You Like It*, II, 7: 'Then a soldier, / Full of strange oaths and bearded like the pard, / Jealous in honour, sudden and quick in quarrel, / Seeking the bubble reputation / Even in the cannon's mouth'.

Augur
The mess corporal mentioned in *Undertones* who was able to provide 'a tempting bottle' from his full box of supplies even under 'a rain of shells' (p. 169).

recite your favourite poem
Alfred Lester (1872–1925) performed in *The Bing Boys* alongside George Robey. Horace (65–8 BC) was known to every schoolboy who had learned Latin, not least for the lines 'Dulce et decorum est pro patria mori' ('How sweet and right it is to die for one's country', *Odes* III.2.13), which in 1913 were inscribed on the wall of the chapel at Sandhurst, the military academy. Wilfred Owen's famous poem of the name, although drafted at Craiglockhart in 1917, was published posthumously in 1920. Harrison, who is speaking here, suggests that Blunden ('Rabbit') recite one of his own poems, having seen the review of his first collection, *Pastorals* (1916), in the *Times Literary Supplement* (*Undertones*, p. 55).

Sergeant Seall
Charles Edward Seall, killed in action in April 1918.

'One Hour of Love with You'
A song written by Worton David with music by Max Darewski, 1917; 'I'd give the sunshine to gaze in your eyes' is a line from the chorus of the same song.

**Fall In, Ghosts**

Massinger's *Bashful Lover*
Philip Massinger (1583–1640), *The Bashful Lover*, a tragicomedy written
in 1636.

'Who were you with last night?'
A song written by Fred Godfrey and Mark Sheridan in 1912: 'Who were
you with last night / Out in the pale moonlight? / Are you going to tell
your Missus / When you get home / Who were you with last night?'

'England was England'
Blunden refers to this song in *Undertones*: 'we had concerts at which the
metre and tune of "England was England when Germany was a pup,"
served for numerous additional verses of personalities' (p. 130).

MMP
Military Mounted Police. During the First World War, the duties of the
MMP included rounding up stragglers, enforcing discipline, dealing
with deserters and duties at courts martial.

Von Krupp
Gustav Krupp von Bolen und Halbach was the head of the German
armaments firm based in Essen.

Alleymans
Germans, from the French *les allemands*.

Fred Worley
Sergeant Frank Worley was the battalion's Wiring Sergeant, of whom
Blunden wrote in *Undertones*: 'A kinder heart there never was: a gentler
spirit never' (p. 45). They remained friends until Worley's death in 1954.

Fontenoy or Malplaquet
The Battle of Fontenoy, 11 May 1745, was a major engagement of the
War of the Austrian Succession, fought between mainly Dutch, British,
and Hanoverian troops under the command of the Duke of Cumber-
land and a French army under Maurice de Saxe, with heavy casualties.
The Battle of Malplaquet, 11 September 1709, was one of the main
battles of the War of the Spanish Succession, and ended in an allied
victory in that the French withdrew and left the field to the Duke of
Marlborough's army. Yet his forces suffered enormous casualties in the
bloodiest battle of the eighteenth century.

V—
A.G. Vidler. Another Old Blue, severely wounded in 1915 near Festubert; later commissioned in the Royal Sussex. Described by Blunden as
'an invincible soldier', he never fully recovered from his head wounds or
the loss of his only brother near Arras in 1917, and committed suicide
in 1924. Blunden's elegy 'A.G.A.V.' is included in *Undertones*.

'household gods plant a terrible fixed foot'
Charles Lamb, 'New Year's Eve' (1821): 'My household gods plant a
terrible fixed foot, and are not rooted up without blood.'

the shadow of a great rock
Isaiah 32:2: 'And a man shall be as a hiding place from the wind and a
covert from the tempest, as rivers of water in a dry place, as the shadow
of a great rock in a weary land.'

'would make themselves air'
William Shakespeare, *Macbeth*, I, 5: 'When I burned in desire / to question them further, they made themselves air, / into which they vanished'.

G.H.H.
Colonel George Hyde Harrison, see above, p. 144.

Mr Davey
'He had been a gentleman's servant and was infallible in courtesy: even
when a shell had just killed two men with him, and he was in a half-dazed
and shocked state, he was correct as at the pay-table.' (Diary entry,
quoted by Webb, *Edmund Blunden*, p. 233.)

Mr Worley
See opposite. Blunden had tried to recommend him for a Victoria Cross.

C.A.U.
Sgt Unsted, perhaps, of whom Blunden writes in *Undertones*: 'The courtesy of Sergeant Unsted, who continued to father No. 11 Platoon, was
charming at every point' (p. 14).

H.T.N.
Blunden refers to him in *Undertones* at Thiepval, on the dangerous St
Martin's Lane: 'it took an experienced messenger, such as our still
smiling runner Norman, four or five hours to come and return' (p. 98).

'a glorious birth'
From William Wordsworth's 'Intimations of Immortality': 'The
sunshine is a glorious birth; / But yet I know, where'er I go, / That there
hath past away a glory from the earth'.

'Come back into memory…'
Charles Lamb, 'Christ's Hospital Five and Thirty Years Ago', in *Essays of Elia* (1823): 'Come back into memory, like as thou wert in the day-spring of thy fancies, with hope like a fiery column before thee – the dark pillar not yet turned – Samuel Taylor Coleridge – Logician, Metaphysician, Bard!'

Daniels
Arthur Edward Daniels, killed in action 31 July 1917; praised by Blunden in 'A Battalion History'.

'has heard more since'
As so often with Blunden, the phrase in its context has a particular relevance: 'I have heard more since. / As flies to wanton boys are we to th' gods. / They kill us for their sport.' – William Shakespeare, *King Lear*, IV, 1.

Bairnsfather's 'Old Bill'
Captain Bruce Bairnsfather (1887–1959) was a cartoonist and humorist, whose weekly 'Fragments from France' cartoons were published in *The Bystander* magazine during the war. They featured Old Bill, a pipe-smoking private in the BEF with a walrus moustache.

Ashford
Sgt W.A. Ashford, 'the bright and clever signaller' often mentioned in *Undertones*; killed in action April 1918.

Clifford
Probably Sergeant Harold Clifford, killed in action 18 September 1917.

E.W. Tice
Also an Old Blue; 'with his stiff, cropped hair he looked an unmistakable German', Blunden wrote in *Undertones*. Five Old Blues went exploring the streets of St Omer in 1917, 'with such exhilarations of wit and irony that we felt no other feast like this could ever come again; nor was the feeling wrong' (p. 148). Tice died of wounds received at St Julien, 1 August 1917.

'None but himself can be his parallel'
Virgil, *Aeneid*, VI, 865: 'quantum instar in ipso'.

Mr de la Mare's haunted forest
Blunden refers to Walter de la Mare's poem 'The Listeners': 'For he suddenly smote on the door, even / Louder, and lifted his head:– / "Tell them I came, and no one answered, / That I kept my word," he said.' It was one of Blunden's favourite poems (Webb, *Edmund Blunden*, p. 248),

along with Shelley's 'The Question' (see below).

a fine excess
'I think poetry should surprise by a fine excess, and not by singularity –
it should strike the reader as a wording of his own highest thoughts, and
appear almost a remembrance'; John Keats to John Taylor, 27 February
1818.

'These see the works of the Lord, and his wonders in the deep'
Psalm 107:24.

## A Battalion History

A battalion was the basic tactical infantry unit of the First World War,
consisting of just over 1,000 men at full strength, of whom 30 were officers. Three battalions were raised by Lieutenant-Colonel Claude
Lowther, MP, in 1914: the 11th, 12th and 13th Battalions of the Royal
Sussex Regiment, known as 1st, 2nd and 3rd Southdown battalions.
These were recruited by voluntary enlistment, but their commanding
officers were regular soldiers with pre-war experience.

Captain Northcote
Edward Stafford Northcote, 1884–1916: 'among the killed were my old
company commanders Penruddock and Northcote (after a great display
of coolness and endurance in the German third line)', *Undertones*, p. 74.

slough of despond
A deep bog in John Bunyan's *The Pilgrim's Progress* (1678).

Trench feet
Frostbite could be the result of standing in freezing cold water; it was not
always treated as a crime, but could be, to make sure that soldiers tried
to prevent it and did not use it as an excuse for malingering.

'looped and ragged nakedness'
William Shakespeare, *King Lear*, III, 4: 'Poor naked wretches, whereso'er
you are, / That bide the pelting of this pitiless storm, / How shall your
houseless heads and unfed sides, / Your loop'd and window'd raggedness, defend you / From seasons such as these?'

Swain
Lieutenant Basil Fitzroy Swain, died in March 1918: 'Fear he respected,
and he exemplified self-conquest' (*Undertones*, p. 7).

'Bare winter suddenly is changed to spring'
P.B. Shelley, 'The Question': 'I dreamed that, as I wandered by the way, / Bare Winter suddenly was changed to Spring'.

## Infantryman Passes By

a very small village in Sussex
Blunden was born in London, but the family moved to the village of Yalding in 1900, where Blunden's father was the schoolmaster. It remained for Blunden the perfect English village. They moved to Framfield in 1913, when Blunden's father was appointed schoolmaster there.

Christ's Hospital
Founded by Edward VI in 1552, the school was for boys 'of honest origin and poverty', described by the poet and essayist Leigh Hunt as 'medium between the patrician pretension of such schools as Eton and Westminster, and the plebian submission of the charity schools... The cleverest boy was the noblest, let his father be who he might.' (See Webb, *Edmund Blunden*, pp. 26–27.)

Lucky boys
Pupils stayed on after 16 if they were judged capable of winning a scholarship to Oxford or Cambridge, and were called 'Grecians' at this stage; Blunden went on to become Senior Grecian or captain of the school. They would usually get a scholarship ('exhibition') from the school as well, so their university education would be at no cost to their parents.

'echoing cloisters pale'
S.T. Coleridge, 'To a Young Lady, with a Poem on the French Revolution', 1794.

'Beat! beat! drums! – blow! bugles! blow!'
Walt Whitman (1819–92) wrote this at the beginning of the American Civil War, in 1861, and it was included in *Leaves of Grass*. It has been set to music by over a dozen composers, including Ralph Vaughan Williams and Kurt Weill.

'the long way to Tipperary'
This music-hall song, 'It's a long, long way to Tipperary', was composed in 1912, and reported as being sung by the Connaught Rangers marching through Boulogne in August 1914. It was widely taken up by other units and further popularised when recorded by John McCormack in November 1914.

a little volume or two
These were *Poems* and *Poems Translated from the French*, both published by
Mr Price of West Street, Horsham, in editions of 100 copies each, priced
at 6d. Webb notes that none of these poems, published in October 1914,
was to be reprinted (*Edmund Blunden*, pp. 39–40).

'What will you lack, sonny, what will you lack'
Blunden is quoting from 'Fall-In', by Harold Begbie (1871–1929), which
appeared on a recruiting poster in 1914. (See http://www.oucs.ox.
ac.uk/ww1lit/gwa/item/5204?CISOBOX=1&REC=10, accessed 2
January 2014.)

the price…of a sword
The first casualty inflicted by the British Army in Europe during WWI
occurred when Captain Charles Hornby of the 4th Royal Irish Dragoon
Guards killed a German uhlan with his sabre, on 22 August 1914. (See
http://www.militarian.com/threads/use-of-the-sword-in-ww1.7075,
accessed 2 January 2014.)

Keats' friend Richards
Probably Charles Richards, who worked as a printer for the firm that
printed Keats's *Poems* (1817); possibly his elder brother, Thomas, who
was a good friend of Charles Cowden Clarke – Blunden wrote about this
circle in his study of Leigh Hunt published in 1930.

'O to recall! / What to recall?'
By Stephen Phillips (1864–1915), *Christ in Hades and Other Poems* (1897),
of which the last stanza runs:

> O to recall!
> What to recall?
> Not the star in waters red,
>    Not this:
> Laughter of a girl that's dead,
>    O this!

'Through the dark postern of time long elapsed'
A much-quoted line from *The Complaint or Night Thoughts on Life, Death and
Immortality* by Edward Young (1683–1765):

> How widow'd every thought of joy!
> Thought, busy thought! Too busy for my peace!
> Through the dark postern of time long elapsed,
> Led softly, by the stillness of the night, […]
> And finds all desert now; and meets the ghosts
> Of my departed joys, a num'rous train!

*Night Thoughts* was one of the books Blunden took to France, and he remarks in *Undertones:* 'I felt the benefit of this grave and intellectual voice, speaking out of a profound eighteenth-century calm, often in metaphor which came home to one even in a pillbox' (p. 170).

'And I live'
Perhaps Edward Young again, 'Who scarce can think it possible, I live? / Alive by miracle!'

''tis the sport to have the engineer…'
William Shakespeare, *Hamlet*, III, 4: 'For 'tis the sport to have the enginer / Hoist with his own petard, and't shall go hard / But I will delve one yard below their mines / And blow them at the moon'.

Marlborough's wars of two centuries before
See notes to 'Fall In, Ghosts', p. 148 above, on Fontenoy and Malplaquet.

Corot's country
Jean-Baptiste-Camille Corot (1796–1875), French landscape painter, who looked back to the neo-Classical tradition and forward to Impressionism. Blunden remarks in *Undertones* that 'while life was nevertheless threatened continually with the last sharp turnings into the unknown, an inestimable sweetness of feeling beyond Corot or Marvell made itself felt through all routine and enforcement' (p. 24).

introduced the tanks
These were first used by the British on the Somme in September 1916, but were slow-moving and difficult to use in the mud.

Wally Ashford
See note to 'Fall In, Ghosts', p. 150 above.

'That agony returns'
S.T. Coleridge, *The Rime of the Ancient Mariner*. 'Since then, at an uncertain hour, / That agony returns; / And till my ghastly tale is told, / This heart within me burns'.

America's armies were in the business
When the Germans resumed their submarine warfare in the Atlantic, and also offered the Mexicans a military alliance, President Wilson asked Congress for a 'war to end all wars' and Congress voted to declare war on 6 April 1917.

'How long, O Lord...'
Psalm 13: 1-2: 'How long wilt thou forget me, O LORD? for ever? How long wilt thou hide thy face from me? / How long shall I take counsel in my soul, having sorrow in my heart daily? How long shall mine enemy be exalted over me?'